THE GOOD, THE BAD, AND THE UGLY
CHICAGO WHITE SOX

HEART-POUNDING, JAW-DROPPING, AND GUT-WRENCHING
MOMENTS FROM CHICAGO WHITE SOX HISTORY

Mark Gonzales

D0368144

TRIUMPH
BOOKS

Copyright © 2009 by Mark Gonzales

No part of this publication may be reproduced, stored in a retrieval system, or transmitted in any form by any means, electronic, mechanical, photocopying, or otherwise, without the prior written permission of the publisher, Triumph Books, 542 South Dearborn Street, Suite 750, Chicago, Illinois 60605.

Triumph Books and colophon are registered trademarks of Random House, Inc.

Library of Congress Cataloging-in-Publication Data

Gonzales, Mark, 1961–
  The good, the bad, and the ugly Chicago White Sox : heart-pounding, jaw-dropping, and gut-wrenching moments from Chicago White Sox history / Mark Gonzales.
    p. cm.
  Includes bibliographical references.
  ISBN 978-1-60078-203-9
  1. Chicago White Sox (Baseball team)—History. 2. Baseball—Illinois—Chicago—History. I. Title.
  GV875.C58G66 2009
  796.357'640977311—dc22
                                                  2008050254

This book is available in quantity at special discounts for your group or organization. For further information, contact:

Triumph Books
542 South Dearborn Street
Suite 750
Chicago, Illinois 60605
(312) 939-3330
Fax (312) 663-3557

Printed in U.S.A.
ISBN: 978-1-60078-203-9
Design by Patricia Frey
Photos courtesy of Mark Fletcher, Tony Inzerillo, Richard C. Lindberg, and Len Maybaum unless otherwise indicated.

CONTENTS

FOREWORD

I used to play baseball on weekends at Brookside Park in Pasadena, right near the Rose Bowl, but I didn't play any baseball in high school. The Dodgers hadn't come to Los Angeles until 1958, so I wasn't a Dodgers fan in 1964. There wasn't any football team, so I spent a lot of my time at the beach. I had very little interest in baseball at all.

But there was an old scout named Hollis "Sloppy" Thurston. I was 17 years old, and he saw me hit three home runs in a game. He offered me $4,000 to sign with the White Sox, then $6,000, then $8,000. I didn't even know what he was talking about. But I needed money to buy books for college—I was trying to go to San Diego State.

The first baseball game I went to with my dad was the 1959 World Series at the Los Angeles Coliseum between the Dodgers and the White Sox. Every kid remembers the first game they go to with their dad, and I remember Luis Aparicio and Nellie Fox. The biggest thrill of my life was signing at 17 and winding up a teammate of Luis Aparicio for a couple of years.

So I've been a Sox fan for more than 50 years. That's the team I rooted for as a kid, and now I've been with them almost 30 years. We've had different ownerships here, from John Allyn to Bill Veeck to Jerry Reinsdorf. But all along, the White Sox have been the team for me.

I got traded to the California Angels in 1975—there were some incidents between me and Harry Caray and I talked to our GM, Roland Hemond, and told him that if they're booing my kids at the father-and-son game and they're booing my wife at the fashion show, there's no sense in me being here. John Allyn was getting ready to sell the ballclub, so dumping my salary was okay with them. But I didn't ask to be traded anywhere specific. Roland said, "I'll trade you home." I didn't find out until later that I was headed to California. I just knew I had to get out of Chicago, even though it was my home away from home. It was just something that had to be done. Then after Anaheim, I went to Cleveland and then into a career in investment real estate with Coldwell Banker.

Finally, I decided that what I really wanted to do was come back and work for the White Sox. Jeff Torborg said I should talk to Jerry, so I came back and met Jerry and told him what I was trying to do.

I'm kind of an outsider looking in, even though I know guys like Greg Walker and Harold Baines and I see them all the time. But they don't remember much about the 1970s, and I don't remember much about the 1980s. But I've always felt like a part of the White Sox, and the feeling of family comes from Jerry Reinsdorf. It didn't have to be a family. But if you play for the White Sox and come through this organization, that is what it is.

Mark Gonzales brings a reflective insight and an honest evaluation of the day-to-day events of the White Sox in this book. It's not all "good," not all "bad," and not all "ugly." It is the perspective of a journalist who brings objectivity to America's pastime, and the city that treasures it. Mark uses his firsthand experience after spending the baseball season traveling city to city with the White Sox, asking the right questions of White Sox players, managers, coaches, and executives. This book shares all of those experiences and interviews with the White Sox fans of Chicago.

—Bill Melton

INTRODUCTION

The Chicago White Sox have definitely experienced their share of the good, the bad, and the ugly in their lengthy history, from starring in one of baseball's biggest scandals to winning the World Series in 2005.

When I started covering baseball on a full-time basis for the *San Jose Mercury News* in 1992, I quickly learned to appreciate the tradition of baseball by listening to the likes of Willie Mays in spring training, and later hearing stories about the game from Bobby Bonds, Mike McCormick, Willie McCovey, and Dusty Baker.

Fast-forward to the present day, and I see revered White Sox greats such as Harold Baines, Greg Walker, and Robin Ventura serving in some capacity. There's definitely a White Sox family when you see former stars like Billy Pierce, Moose Skowron, and Ron Kittle at U.S. Cellular Field, SoxFest, or a worthwhile function.

In 1984, a childhood friend told me about one of his teammates, a chatty kid playing shortstop for the Triple-A Las Vegas Stars. That teammate was Ozzie Guillen.

Through all the second-place finishes and nonchampionship seasons, a bond still exists throughout the White Sox's organization, the same way it does within the San Francisco Giants organization that I followed as a kid and later covered.

But with general manager Kenny Williams, a Bay Area native whom I was lucky enough to cover when he was a two-sport standout at Mount Pleasant High School in San Jose, the White Sox's objective remains singular.

Winning.

The task and challenges of accomplishing that feat, through baseball's endless potholes and gold mines, remains fascinating to a long-standing franchise and its thousands of followers.

DON'T STOP BELIEVIN' AFTER 88 YEARS

After four consecutive seasons without a division title, White Sox general manager Kenny Williams knew he had to infuse a plodding roster with pitching and speed to have any chance of knocking off perennial American League Central nemesis Minnesota before the 2005 season.

But midway through the winter meetings at the Anaheim Marriott, Williams had already struck out twice in attempts to reshape an underachieving, injury-plagued team.

He aimed high immediately, starting with his pursuit of free agent Gold Glove shortstop Omar Vizquel only to be trumped at the last minute by San Francisco, which was willing to give Vizquel a guaranteed third year that swayed him away from the White Sox.

Undaunted, Williams asked Arizona about the availability of Randy Johnson, a five-time Cy Young Award winner who was interested in pitching for a contender following the Diamondbacks' 111-loss season. But after Arizona asked for staff ace Mark Buehrle and Freddy Garcia in return, Williams quickly shifted gears.

Williams was determined to improve the White Sox's speed, pitching, and defense. He left the winter meetings with speedy but injury-prone leadoff batter Scott Podsednik and resilient reliever Luis Vizcaino. It came at the cost of slugger Carlos Lee, but it gave Williams the flexibility to make more moves by eliminating Lee's $8 million salary.

While scouting an Arizona Fall League game in November with assistant Dave Wilder, Williams ran into agent Casey Close. Williams and Close moved to a secluded area of Scottsdale Stadium and began talking about free-agent pitcher Dustin Hermanson, who showed his versatility with San Francisco by agreeing to move to the closer role for the final two months of 2004.

After meeting with Hermanson at a pizza restaurant he owned a share of in North Phoenix, Williams reached a two-year deal to help fortify the bullpen.

Nine days later, the Sox made a small move that would pay great dividends by claiming flamethrowing but unpolished pitcher Bobby Jenks from the Los Angeles Angels organization with the intent to groom him as a future closer at Double-A Birmingham.

Williams signed postseason pitching veteran Orlando "El Duque" Hernandez to be his fifth starter and to make fellow Cuban Jose Contreras feel more comfortable. After thoroughly talking to several sources, Williams also signed left-handed-hitting catcher A.J. Pierzynski, who was run out of San Francisco after only one season.

Perhaps Williams' best signing was his most curious. Relying on videotape as much as scouting reports, he signed Tadahito Iguchi to start at second base after eight modest seasons in Japan without the marquee hoopla of fellow countrymen Ichiro Suzuki and Hideo Nomo.

Rarely do new ingredients blend so well so quickly. The Sox went wire-to-wire to win their first American League Central title since 2000 with one of the wildest rides in recent history.

The crusade began April 4 when Mark Buehrle allowed only two hits over eight innings in a 1–0 Opening Day victory over Cleveland.

The Sox posted an American League–best 17–7 record in April, went 18–10 in May, and went a league-best 18–7 in June.

Thanks to Podsednik, the White Sox outscored their opponents 121–68 in the first inning, with the 121 runs representing the most in the first inning by any team in the majors that season.

The White Sox also ran off three eight-game winning streaks before July 1, becoming just the fifth team in the majors to accomplish this since 1900, according to the Elias Sports Bureau. And Buehrle earned the victory in the All-Star Game at Detroit that gave the American League home-field advantage in the World Series.

After the break, the White Sox swept division foe Cleveland in a four-game series to start the second half and had a seemingly commanding 15-game lead on August 1.

While much of the July 31 trade talk focused on Ken Griffey Jr. and Florida free-agent-to-be pitcher A.J. Burnett, Williams performed only some small fine-tuning by landing switch-hitting infielder Geoff Blum from San Diego for a minor league pitcher.

The White Sox's lead, however, shrunk to 8½ games after a seven-game losing streak in mid-August. They maintained a 9½-game lead with 24 contests left, but a four-game losing streak suddenly cut the lead to 5½ games, and reliever Damaso Marte was asked to leave the team for a brief period after breaking one of manager Ozzie Guillen's rules.

The lead was cut to 1½ games with 10 games left following a 4–1 home loss to Minnesota. Suddenly, the Sox had to rely on Contreras, whose lack of development caused the New York Yankees to trade him in the middle of the 2004 season, to direct them to the finish line.

Contreras beat the Twins the following night to help the Sox embark on a three-game winning streak. They didn't gain any ground on Cleveland, but the Sox regained their confidence under duress. Despite losing two games at Detroit, the Sox were finally benefiting from a long-awaited cool-off by Cleveland.

After embarking on a 43–15 run, the Indians lost at Kansas City, then dropped two straight at home to Tampa Bay while the Sox dropped a pair at Detroit.

"We feel like, 'What's going to be next?'" Guillen said. "I think someone has to step up and grab this team by the horns and take charge."

Contreras snapped the Sox's skid with an 8–2 win over the Tigers, and the Sox found out before their series finale at Comerica Park that a victory would give them the AL Central title.

The final out wasn't made until first baseman Paul Konerko squeezed Placido Polanco's line drive with the tying run at first. It came shortly after Konerko had a brief disagreement with coach Joey Cora over where to play Polanco.

"I wanted to move over to the left because I didn't want a double to tie the game," Konerko said. "I argued with Joey, who said to stay where I was. It was hit right at me. The last three weeks, the reverse of that was happening.

"If you said before the season that we were going to win the division, you're lying," said Konerko, who kept the ball from the last out in his locker.

Elation and relief steered the Sox's cigar-and-champagne-reeking bus drive from Detroit to Cleveland, where they were to play a three-game series against the Indians.

It also was a crazy time for third baseman Joe Crede, who returned in time to be on the field for the final out after missing two games to attend the birth of his daughter Lucy Renee.

Shortly after arriving in Cleveland, the Sox's traveling party received a big surprise. Frank Thomas, who hadn't played since July 20 after reinjuring his foot, threw a party for his teammates.

"It was good," Thomas said later. "I had been there a long time and had been through some struggles. I saw the organization when I got there, and to get to that level...it was assumed, but it was a long haul. It was the least I could do, because we were reaching where we wanted to be."

The party gave Guillen another reason to rest his regulars and start his reserves against a Cleveland team still fighting for a playoff spot. With a blend of benchwarmers and regulars, the Sox knocked Cleveland out of playoff contention with a three-game sweep.

Guillen took great delight at the expense of his critics after his reserves finished off the Indians in a 13-inning 3–2 win after a Ross Gload double.

"People were killing me because I don't respect the game," Guillen said. "They only worry about it because it was Boston and

New York [in contention]. I did what every manager in baseball does. After you clinch, you always play the bench guys.

"But Ozzie Guillen did it and he's stupid and ignorant and doesn't know about baseball. Bobby Cox does it and he's a genius. Even when I win, I can't win. I want to win more than anyone else.

"Sometimes I just laugh at people's comments. People think I just got here, like this is my first playoff I've ever been to."

Clinching the division and home-field advantage throughout the playoffs gave the Sox time to set their rotation and postseason roster before their Division Series matchup with Boston.

The Sox routed Boston 14–2 in the first game, and then took advantage of Tony Graffanino's error and rode Tadahito Iguchi's grand slam off David Wells to a 5–4 win in Game 2.

The Sox were looking for the sweep in Game 3 while also trying to avoid facing Red Sox ace Curt Schilling in a possible Game 4. The Sox were in danger of heading in that direction after a heavily perspired Freddy Garcia threw 98 pitches and was pulled in the sixth inning after allowing a leadoff home run to Manny Ramirez that cut the lead to 4–3.

Marte loaded the bases on a single and two walks, with Pierzynski firing the ball back to the mound and glaring into the dugout after each errant pitch.

That set the stage for Orlando Hernandez to salvage his injury-plagued season.

Once destined to be a spectator, Hernandez pitched his way onto the postseason roster by throwing a scoreless inning in the Sox's 12-inning win over the Indians during the season's final week, then hurling two scoreless innings two days later.

So Guillen summoned Hernandez, a Cuban defector who thrived on pitching on baseball's biggest stages as evidenced by his 9–3 postseason record with the New York Yankees.

Hernandez induced pinch-hitter Jason Varitek to foul out to first and Tony Graffanino to pop to short after a 10-pitch at-bat.

That set up a showdown with Johnny Damon, Boston's single-slapping left-handed hitter. But Hernandez teased Damon to chase a breaking pitch before he could check his swing, and umpire Mark

Wegner called Damon out as the Sox ran off the field like children leaving their final day of elementary school.

"I know this kid is going to show up with cold blood," Guillen said after Hernandez helped the Sox advance to the ALCS with a 5–3 win.

Guillen got the highest praise—from chairman Jerry Reinsdorf—over the decision to carry Hernandez on the roster.

"I was hoping we could get out of it [giving up just one] run," a champagne-soaked Reinsdorf said. "I have to give Ozzie credit. There was very serious debate whether El Duque was on the roster, but Ozzie and Don Cooper wanted him and Kenny Williams deferred to them. He came up big."

The Sox's three days off before Game 1 of the AL Championship Series proved to be little advantage as the Los Angeles Angels flew all night after knocking out the Yankees in the other ALDS and beat the Sox 3–2 behind the crafty pitching of Paul Byrd.

Game 2 looked nearly as tough for the Sox as A.J. Pierzynski swung and missed at a Kelvim Escobar pitch with two out in the bottom of the ninth inning and the score tied 1–1.

Pierzynski started toward the Sox dugout but, like an option quarterback, reversed his course and ran toward first base as Angels catcher Josh Paul (who entered the game in the bottom of the eighth) rolled the ball back to the mound as his teammates headed toward the first-base dugout.

Pierzynski reached base safely, and home-plate umpire Doug Eddings ruled that Paul never caught Escobar's third strike. That set off a firestorm of anger from the Angels well after Joe Crede ripped a game-winning double down the left-field line to score pinch runner Pablo Ozuna and give the Sox a 2–1 win and the momentum.

The irony is that Paul was born near Chicago and grew up rooting for the White Sox and was eventually drafted by them in 1996.

Despite playing the next three games at Angel Stadium, the Sox's confidence was in their starting pitching. And it proved well placed, as Jon Garland (pitching on 12 days' rest), Freddy Garcia, and Jose Contreras each pitched complete-game victories that sent the Sox to the World Series for the first time since 1959.

Fittingly, pitching coach Don Cooper and each of the Sox's starters posed on the Angels' mound with bottles of champagne and cigars to celebrate their conquest.

With five days before Game 1 of the World Series, the Sox took two days off before gradually getting back into game shape and even holding simulated games for their starting pitchers who had received an extended break.

A.J. Pierzynski was awarded first base after striking out against the Angels' Kelvim Escobar in Game 2 of the 2005 ALCS. Photo courtesy of AP Images.

Their final opponent was Houston, making its first World Series appearance in franchise history. The Astros had a mixture of veterans—like aging Cy Young Award winner Roger Clemens, Jeff Bagwell, and Craig Biggio—and promising stars—like first baseman Lance Berkman, closer Brad Lidge, and third baseman Morgan Ensberg.

"A lot of people should enjoy it," Buehrle said at the time. "Growing up as a baseball fan, I kind of got tired seeing the same teams in the World Series."

The Sox scored three runs in the first two innings of Game 1 against Clemens, who aggravated his hamstring under damp conditions. Contreras wasn't as dominant as he had been in the past, but he earned the victory as Crede hit a tie-breaking home run in the fourth in a 5–3 win.

The final three innings of Game 2 rank as some of the most memorable highlights in Sox history. Trailing 4–2, Paul Konerko ripped Chad Qualls' first pitch into the left-field seats for a grand slam in the seventh that gave the Sox the lead that stood until rookie closer Bobby Jenks allowed a two-out, two-run, pinch-hit single to Jose Vizcaino in the ninth.

As temperatures dipped into the low 40s, the thought of a home run seemed unlikely, especially to a batter like Scott Podsednik—who had not hit a home run in 507 regular-season at-bats—and especially off Astros closer Brad Lidge.

"Walking up to the plate, I was thinking more along the lines of slapping a base hit to left and stealing second," Podsednik revealed later.

But the slender Podsednik ripped a Lidge pitch high and deep to right center that seemed to guile its way over the fence, sending a soggy U.S. Cellular Field crowd into delirium.

"I didn't think it would be that quick or on a homer by him," Konerko said.

It was the perfect sendoff for Podsednik, who grew up 200 miles outside of Houston and was returning to his home state for Games 3 and 4.

"It's pretty indescribable," said Podsednik, who had recently become engaged to model-actress Lisa Dergan.

Paul Konerko's grand slam off Astros reliever Chad Qualls in Game 2 of the 2005 World Series sent Sox fans into a frenzy. Photo courtesy of Getty Images.

Scott Podsednik's game-winning home run off Astros closer Brad Lidge cemented his place in White Sox history. Photo courtesy of AP Images.

The bat that Podsednik used to hit the home run was later delivered to the National Baseball Hall of Fame in Cooperstown, New York.

"That's pretty special," Podsednik said. "If that doesn't define irony, I don't know what does."

During the Sox's off-day workout at Minute Maid Park, Buehrle placed his valuable left arm in a basket of ice. He was in obvious discomfort but wasn't scheduled to pitch again unless there was a Game 6 back in Chicago.

Little did anyone know how badly Buehrle would be needed.

Against Roy Oswalt, the Astros' best pitcher, the Sox found themselves down 4–0 after four innings in Game 3. But as they did in Game 2 of the ALDS, the Sox proved a four-run deficit wasn't insurmountable. They rallied on Joe Crede's home run and A.J. Pierzynski's two-run double to take a 5–4 lead. Emotions ran deeper after Oswalt drilled Crede with a pitch, prompting Crede to stare into the Astros dugout.

Houston manager Phil Garner, no favorite of White Sox GM Kenny Williams, yelled at Crede. That prompted designated hitter Carl Everett, who was resigned to bench duty in Houston because NL parks don't employ the DH, to climb to the top of the dugout steps to scream at Garner.

"It's best that I don't talk about Phil Garner," Williams said the next day. "I had problems with him even before he said those things about my players, and it's just best kept between the two of us. I have no reason or desire to speak to him about anything."

The Sox got the last laugh, as Garner's emotions grew louder on baseball's biggest stage.

Houston tied the game in their half of the eighth before the game went into extra innings. Reserve Geoff Blum entered the game as part of a double-switch in the bottom of the thirteenth, but his bat became more important than his defense.

In the top of the fourteenth, Blum dropped the barrel of his bat on a pitch from rookie Ezequiel Astacio and hit it into the right-field seats to give the Sox a 6–5 lead.

"It's the stuff dreams are made of," said Blum, whose wife had given birth to twin girls earlier that season while playing for San Diego. "I've had about a hundred of these at-bats in my backyard with my younger brother. But to do it on this stage and in this situation makes this year incredibly worthwhile."

Television cameras caught Garner heaving a chair into the dugout tunnel.

With closer Bobby Jenks already out of the game, the Sox called upon Buehrle to get the final out with the tying runs on base.

"I wasn't hurt that bad not to pitch," Buehrle said. "I asked [Don Cooper] as the game went along in the seventh or eighth inning. We used a few guys less than an inning and went through the bullpen. I think [Cooper] got sick of me asking him from the tenth inning on. Finally he said, 'Go ahead, get out of here and get your cleats on.' I think he did that just to get me out of the dugout.

"The next thing you know, they said if certain guys get on, you're going in the game. I don't think they planned on using me. I think they did it just to say, 'Quit bugging me, get away and go down there. We're not going to use you.'"

Of all the Opening Day, All-Star Game, and postseason starts, this assignment felt like no other to Buehrle.

"It was the most nervous I've been coming in a game," he said. "The last time I threw out of the bullpen was 2000, and here I was in the World Series. The last thing I remember is opening the bullpen door. I don't remember running in. I remember hearing Sox employees cheering from the upper deck."

In Game 4, Freddy Garcia pitched seven shutout innings against the team that traded him to Seattle to get Randy Johnson back in 1998. Willie Harris, who lost his starting job at second to Iguchi, led off the eighth with a pinch-hit single and reached third with two outs.

On a 1–1 count, Jermaine Dye bounced a single up the middle off Brad Lidge to give the Sox a 1–0 lead.

With little margin for error, Guillen called on Jenks for the fourth consecutive game despite a left oblique muscle pull that Jenks endured throughout the entire postseason.

"I felt it, but once you got loose, the adrenaline of the situation...I had it all through the playoffs. It was one of those things, you don't remember that you're sore," Jenks said.

Besides, after getting waived by the Los Angeles Angels less than 12 months ago, Jenks had a chance to complete one of the most amazing turnarounds for his team and himself after vaulting from Double-A Birmingham in early July.

"I knew I had a shot, especially with the way I was throwing," said Jenks, who had a 2.85 ERA with 19 saves in 35 appearances for the Barons. "Razor Shines was our manager. I had a conversation before a game and I thought he was joking when he said he thought I had a chance to be called up by [that] Wednesday.

"I didn't realize the day he told me was a Wednesday. I was really surprised. Everything happened so quick. I was called up before the All-Star break. Everything was thrown at me all at once, and I think that helped me in different situations."

This situation, however, was more urgent. Generations of White Sox fans sensed an opportunity for the ultimate celebration and didn't want to wait any longer.

With the tying run at second, shortstop Juan Uribe made two signature plays that made White Sox fans temporarily forget about his tendency to swing wildly at breaking pitches. Uribe sprinted toward the left-field line and leaned over the railing to catch Chris Burke's foul pop for the second out. The final batter, pinch-hitter Orlando Palmeiro, hit a grounder past the left side of the mound that Jenks couldn't field. But Uribe charged and threw quickly to first to barely nail Palmeiro and set off a celebration that lasted more than an hour on the Minute Maid infield.

"It all went by so quick," said Jenks, who was embraced by Pierzynski before a major pileup occurred near the mound. "I had to look at video to remember all the pitches I threw. It was just a blur at the time."

Chairman Jerry Reinsdorf, flanked by several White Sox front-office staffers and family members, shook his head in amazement as he scooted past reporters in a corridor leading to the field.

Reinsdorf hoisted the World Series trophy on the mound and posed for seemingly endless photographs with several supporters and even a few media members.

With the World Series victory, Reinsdorf became only the third owner to win titles in two of the four major sports, joining Jack Kent Cooke (Los Angeles Lakers and Washington Redskins) and Bill Davidson (Detroit Pistons and Tampa Bay Lightning).

"In sports, I haven't had a greater feeling," said Williams, completing one of the most remarkable rebuilding projects in Chicago history.

It also granted a sense of gratification to several Sox players who didn't have the marquee billing that Astros like Roger Clemens, Jeff Bagwell, or Craig Biggio had. The Sox also lacked the playoff allure that Boston or the New York Yankees possessed.

"We never had any egos on this team," said Dye, who joined the Sox as a free agent from Oakland and replaced Magglio Ordonez. "I think that was what was really special about this club."

It was quite a 24 hours for Roland Hemond, who was serving as an executive adviser to Williams. Hemond turned 76 years old shortly before Blum hit his game-winning home run in Game 3. His wife, Margo, gave him a kiss as a birthday present. That buzz on the lips was seen on national television, and Hemond and his wife embraced again after the final out was made in Game 4 roughly 23 hours later.

The White Sox held a party at their hotel that lasted well past 3:00 AM, with some media members unsuccessfully trying to crash the event.

"Enjoy it and be safe," Konerko said before heading to the party.

"To beat Boston, get four consecutive complete games against the Angels, and then beat Houston in four, that's a cherry on top," pitching coach Don Cooper said. "I'm going to celebrate and enjoy this until next spring training."

With one day to recuperate, the White Sox looked refreshed as they were hailed throughout various Chicago neighborhoods before they completed their parade celebration at La Salle Street and Wacker Drive.

"That might have been the coolest off-the-field event I'd ever seen," Jenks said. "Seeing that many people downtown and rolling through the city."

Thousands of fans gathered in downtown Chicago to celebrate an event many never thought they'd live to see: a White Sox World Series championship. Photo courtesy of AP Images.

MR. OCTOBER

Playing without a contract past 2005 didn't weigh on Paul Konerko in the second half of that season as he helped carry the White Sox to the 2005 American League Central title with a .323 batting average, 20 home runs, and 45 RBIs after the All-Star break.

As the playoffs got closer, Konerko had bigger issues. His wife, Jennifer, was scheduled to deliver the couple's first child, Nicholas, in late October.

"We knew it could be a possibility," Konerko recalled. "I don't think we knew in spring training that we were going to the World Series, but September moved in and then we were in the playoffs. And when the playoffs started, it became a possibility."

As the White Sox advanced further into the playoffs, Konerko's stock grew as a free agent and speculation grew that he could end up joining the team he helped eliminate in the American League Championship Series—the Los Angeles Angels—because of his association with manager Mike Scioscia dating from his minor league days with the Dodgers. Anaheim was also just an hour flight from Konerko's Phoenix-area home.

But Konerko couldn't wait to get out of Anaheim and back home once the White Sox beat the Angels in five games, giving the Sox plenty of time to rest and prepare for the World Series.

And it gave Konerko the perfect break to join his wife.

"It couldn't have worked out any better because her due date was during the World Series and on a game day, but we just decided to have that baby in between [the ALCS and the World Series]. I was thinking when were up 3–1, *What if I have to leave and not be here for the World Series and be faced with that question?*

"Once we had that baby in between, it was a little weight off my shoulders. You still have to play the World Series and it's a big deal. But at that point, you're on autopilot. You've played so many games, starting from spring training. At that point, you're playing on sheer adrenaline."

After the birth of Nick, Konerko returned to Chicago to resume preparations.

"It was draining, but I don't think any of us thought about it," Konerko said. "We just kept pushing and pushing until it was over. I guess that's why it's so tough to win."

The Sox had the benefit of opening every postseason series at home by virtue of having the AL's best regular-season record (99–63). But they were in danger of losing that advantage until Konerko came to the plate against Houston reliever Chad Qualls in Game 2 with the Sox trailing 4–2 in the seventh and the bases loaded.

"First pitch, all I remember thinking about before I went up there was that we were down 4–2," Konerko recalled. "I just kept telling myself to be ready for the first pitch, that a single could tie the game. Don't try to do too much. Stay up the middle because a base hit could tie this game. Don't do anything more, but I did more."

A blue seat near the White Sox's bullpen now stands out like a sore thumb, but that seat remains among the sea of forest green seats to commemorate the spot where Konerko's grand slam landed. Although the Astros came back with a ninth-inning rally before Scott Podsednik hit his game-winning home run in the bottom of the ninth, Konerko's homer ranks as one of the greatest moments in franchise history.

"I remember the place was electric after that, even after we took the field," Konerko recalled. "When we took the field in the top of the eighth, just because there were longer delays because of TV, when I was rolling ground balls to guys, it was just so electric. Losing that lead and coming back, considering the weather, it was a pretty amazing game."

Konerko wonders how much strength the White Sox had left had Houston won Game 4.

"That whole three weeks of the playoffs, it didn't even feel like we slept at all," he said. "I remember being so tired when it was over. You don't think about it when it's going on.

"We clinched the ALCS quickly and had five days off, so it gave me some time to situate things. I just remember when it was over, after we won in Houston, we celebrated on the field, but I remember at the hotel I didn't have anything left to give. I couldn't celebrate any more. I just wanted to go home and sleep back home in Arizona."

After assessing his free-agent options with reporters in the players' parking lot at U.S. Cellular Field, Konerko and the White Sox went on a double-decker bus ride through several neighborhoods that they'll always relish.

"Of all the things that went on during the playoffs, that was the biggest surprise," Konerko said. "We really didn't think about that thing until we won. But I don't think anyone envisioned what went on with the parade. We went through all the streets around the ballpark and saw nice crowds, and it definitely would have been good, just with that. But when we went downtown and saw that many people...."

"We didn't have time to think about or even talk about what the parade was going to be like. We won in Houston, and the next thing you know, we're on buses. You just kind of get going. It blew everyone away.

"People have seen the Bears and Bulls [win championships], but as far as baseball, it had been so long since they won one, I don't think anyone knew what to expect. We didn't. It really blew us away."

Five weeks later, the party continued. After intense negotiations that involved Baltimore and the Los Angeles Angels, Konerko signed a five-year, $60 million extension with the White Sox.

QUIT NOW?

Throughout his tenure as White Sox manager, Ozzie Guillen has spoken frankly about walking away.

Never did he seem as serious as he did in late September 2005, with the Sox trying not to blow all of a 15-game lead in the American League Central.

Guillen was fed up with the booing from his own fans, adding that he was vomiting often from the stress and was feeling unappreciated. Winning the World Series would allow him to get out on top of the baseball world and not be subjected to the second-guessing.

"I've got [championship] rings already and I'm proud of them, but if I win here, if I help the White Sox do this, it will give me a chance to walk away if I want to," Guillen told Mike Nadel of the Copley News Service before the White Sox suffered an 8–0 loss to Cleveland that cut their lead to 2½ games.

"I will think about it. I will think about it twice. The way I'm thinking right now, I will tell Kenny Williams to get another manager and I'll get the [bleep] out of here. I'll make more money signing autographs instead of dealing with this [bleep]."

Guillen was asked to clarify his comments, and he sounded even more convincing.

"I'm not kidding, not at all," Guillen said. "I want the fans to be able to say, 'Hey, we finally did it!' I want to make them proud. I want to win the World Series, and then maybe I'm gone. I'll even help Kenny look for someone else.

"I don't give a [bleep] about the money; I've got all I need. The thing is, I'm stressed every day. Do I have the best job in the world? Yes, because I'm managing the team I love. I'm managing my team. But every time we lose, I feel sick. I [vomit] sometimes. I get mad. I throw things in my office. It makes me crazy.

"I went to the World Series as a player [with Atlanta] and won one as a coach [with Florida]. If I can do it as the manager here, I can say, 'Everything I want to do in baseball, I did it.' Then I'll make my decision."

The criticism hurt Guillen most because he played 13 seasons for the White Sox and came back to manage but didn't feel the loyalty from the fans was reciprocated, adding that he has "30,000 managers helping me out."

"It makes me sad when they boo me," he said. "Sometimes I think they don't appreciate me. They should, because I played my [bleep] off for them and now I'm managing my [bleep] off for them. You know how many managers are dying for 91 wins right now? And we have that and they don't appreciate that? It makes me wonder what happens if I only have 71 wins, how are they gonna treat me? I mean, they treat me like [bleep] when I'm winning 91.

"My kids are here at the ballpark and they ask me later why I'm getting booed. I say it's part of my job, but deep down inside, it hurts. If I was doing a [bleep] job, sure, go ahead and boo me, but I think I'm doing pretty good."

Five weeks later, after the White Sox won the World Series, Guillen told beat writers he'd have some news for them.

That turned out to be the news that he was returning.

THE PARTY'S OVER

Less than a month after watching the White Sox win their first World Series title in 88 years, GM Kenny Williams started to reconstruct the roster in a manner that stunned several faithful fans.

No move was more emotional than the trading of center fielder and fan favorite Aaron Rowand to Philadelphia, along with minor league pitchers Gio Gonzalez and Daniel Haigwood, for future Hall of Fame slugger Jim Thome.

About three weeks prior to the trade, the Sox said good-bye to prolific hitter Frank Thomas. Those wheels were in motion when Thomas, out with a foot injury that limited him to 34 games in 2005, threw the ceremonial first pitch before Game 1 of the American League Division Series.

A week after addressing the crowd at the World Series parade, the White Sox gave Thomas a $3.5 million buyout.

That irked Thomas, who expressed his disappointment to *Daily Southtown* columnist Phil Arvia while training with his new Oakland team in spring training in Phoenix.

"I've got a lot of respect for Jerry Reinsdorf, I do," Thomas told Arvia. "But I really thought, the relationship we had over the last 16 years, he would have picked up the phone to say, 'Big guy, we're moving forward. We're going somewhere different. We don't know your situation or what's going to happen.' I can live with that. I really can.

"But treating me like some passing-by player, I got no respect for that."

Knocking Reinsdorf is a cardinal sin in Williams' eyes, and he fired back in one of his sharpest responses since becoming GM.

"More upsetting to me than his comments directed at me are the comments directed at the organization and at Jerry

Reinsdorf," Williams told reporters in the White Sox's media workroom in Tucson. "Jerry doesn't deserve that, particularly with regards to Frank. Jerry has done everything over the course of 16 years to protect that man, to make accommodations for him, concessions for him. He loaned him money, at times, when he needed money. And for him to forget that, for him to turn his back on all that, it's a crying shame."

After a long pause, Williams barked, "Next question."

But the responses continued, getting longer and more pointed.

"Let me tell you something. There are a lot of guys around here that have been with the White Sox organization, I'm one of them and damn near all of my coaches, for 20 some odd years. Jerry is almost, he is like a second father to a lot of us. For these back-handed comments, actually they aren't even back-handed anymore. They are full frontal smashes right in our face. For these to keep coming, and again, for him to turn his back on all the things Jerry has done. And this guy? This guy, of all people? Please."

As for Thomas' regret about throwing out the first pitch and not addressing the fans before getting his buyout, Williams threw a verbal roundhouse punch.

"He's an idiot," Williams said. "He's selfish. That's why we don't miss him. And we've held it in for far too long. And if you go out there and look long and hard enough, you will find particulars."

Williams and Thomas talked via phone later that night and agreed to disagree.

"I think that was very immature on his part to even bring that up," Thomas told the *Daily Southtown*. "Jerry had done a lot of wonderful things for me over the years. I have a great relationship with Jerry Reinsdorf. I think the comments were more toward Jerry Reinsdorf and not out of disrespect. I don't think [Williams] had to sit there and respond on Jerry's behalf. I have no animosity toward Jerry Reinsdorf. We had a great relationship. We'll move forward eventually in the future. As for responding to all of this, it's all a bunch of noise.

"I went through a very public divorce. He helped me out in a spot there, but it was nothing more than a loan. It was more of my contract. That was just a nasty situation in '99 and 2000. We've been way past that a long time ago."

Thomas' buyout overshadowed the same move the White Sox made with designated hitter Carl Everett, also known as "the Truth."

Everett landed in Seattle as the Mariners' DH and made a trek to Tucson for a series of exhibition games. Before a game against the White Sox, Everett was asked whether his former team could defend its world championship, especially with the mass changes made in the off-season.

"Being me and being honest," Everett said near the visitor's dugout at Tucson Electric Park, "I'm going to say, no, they can't repeat. They are not going to have the same chemistry. A lot of the chemistry in that clubhouse is gone. Rowand, myself, even Willie [Harris] and Frank. We all had a presence in there and now the new guys will have to fit in. You are bringing in guys to fit in."

When asked if the team's leadership was still there, Everett said, "No."

Everett also wasn't sure if the White Sox had anyone besides manager Ozzie Guillen who could step up during tough times.

"You don't have any voices in there to say, 'Hey, let's get this going,'" Everett said. "Thome is a nice guy, but I think Thome will be feeling around first. They have a nice team, but at the same time, who knows?

"It's a great squad. But it will surprise you who will be the voice in that clubhouse that nobody expected—A.J. [Pierzynski]. A.J. will be the voice. People won't think about that, but he will be the voice."

Everett also questioned Paul Konerko's appointment as team captain, a title Konerko reluctantly accepted.

"No, he's not vocal," Everett said. "Neither was Frank, but I considered him one of the leaders. That captain stuff is overrated. I would never pick one guy as a captain. I wouldn't want that pressure on me. I wouldn't want to wear the 'C' on my shoulder. No.

I mean, you see guys are wearing that thing reluctantly. That should stay in hockey."

When informed of Everett's comments, Williams had a spirited discussion with Everett—with Williams doing most of the talking—outside the team's clubhouse.

2008: A LESSON IN PERSEVERANCE

S harp-fielding third baseman Joe Crede played less than two-thirds of the season because of recurring back pain. Paul Konerko suffered one of his worst seasons at the plate while coping with nagging injuries. Fellow slugger Jim Thome batted a full-season career-low .245. Nick Swisher, whom the White Sox acquired from Oakland in exchange for three prospects, batted .219 and possessed only a .332 on-base percentage.

Jerry Owens, who was projected as the White Sox's leadoff hitter entering spring training, suffered a groin injury and didn't get brought back until September. Valuable set-up reliever Scott Linebrink missed nearly two months because of tendinitis behind his right shoulder. Starting pitcher Jose Contreras missed the final several weeks because of an Achilles tendon tear.

And despite all these mishaps, in 2008 the White Sox won their second American League Central title in four seasons.

To say they did this the hard way would be one of the all-time understatements in White Sox history. Despite leading the division for 148 days, the White Sox fell out of first place after getting swept at Minnesota in a three-game series September 23–25. Even chairman Jerry Reinsdorf later admitted that he felt the White Sox had missed their chance at winning the division title.

The White Sox's only losing month occurred in September, when they were 12–15. But they were aided by the concurrent struggles of division rival Minnesota prior to their three-game debacle at the Metrodome, where they were only 1–8. (In fact, the Sox won the division despite posting a major league–worst 4–16 record in domes.)

So how did they pull out a division title and amass 89 victories?

For starters, pitchers Gavin Floyd and John Danks, who entered 2008 with only 55 major league starts between them, combined for 29 victories. Both pitchers were acquired after the 2006 season and represent two of general manager Kenny Williams' finest moves, despite the instant criticism that came after trading big-game veteran Freddy Garcia and rising star pitcher Brandon McCarthy.

Another acquisition that paid off immediately was trading for outfielder Carlos Quentin, who nearly didn't make the Opening Day roster until Owens was placed on the 15-day disabled list.

After the offense got off to a sputtering start, manager Ozzie Guillen moved No. 2 hitter Orlando Cabrera (acquired from the Los Angeles Angels during the off-season for Jon Garland) to the leadoff spot on May 5, and Cabrera batted .293 from there, including a .353 mark in his final 17 games.

Nine days later, Guillen moved Quentin to the third spot, and his production became more recognizable with Thome and Konerko continuing to struggle. And after second baseman Juan Uribe suffered a hamstring pull in Anaheim on May 15, the bottom of the order was fortified by Alexei Ramirez, who was kept on the Opening Day roster despite having no previous professional experience in the United States after leaving Cuba the previous fall.

Ramirez was nicknamed "the Cuban Missile" for his quick bat and speed, and he set a major league record for rookies by hitting four grand slams in addition to his .290 batting average, 21 home runs, and 71 RBIs. Ramirez was also fifth in the AL with a .380 batting average with runners in scoring position.

With the comfort of a two-year contract, veteran right fielder Jermaine Dye rebounded from a down year with a .292 batting average, 34 home runs, and 96 RBIs.

Catcher A.J. Pierzynski, who received a two-year extension at the end of the White Sox's disastrous 2007 season, embarked on a

Alexei Ramirez hit .290, drove in 77 runs, and finished second in the AL Rookie of the Year balloting in 2008. Photo courtesy of AP Images.

weight-loss program that paid off handsomely. Playing 20 pounds lighter, Pierzynski legged out many of his 31 doubles, caught at least 1,000 innings for the seventh consecutive season, and batted .286 against left-handed pitchers. His batting average hovered close to the .300 mark until the final month of the season.

A White Sox season wouldn't be complete without its share of amusement and controversy. Swisher added spark to a stoic group of veterans by riding a minibike through the spring-training clubhouse in Tucson, distributed "Dirty 30" T-shirts (an homage to his playing style and uniform number) to his teammates, and expanded the charity group that he started in Oakland. But turnabout was fair play: before a game at Cleveland, Swisher and teammate Brian Anderson fell victim to the three-man pull—one of the oldest pranks in baseball—in which players are tangled on the ground and subject to clubhouse-spread leftovers and other debris.

Other controversies lingered throughout the season. For example, it's common for a player or coach to call the press box to ask an official scorer to review a call he might not agree with. Pitching coach Don Cooper called the Wrigley Field press box asking Bob Rosenberg to take a second look at a call following a 7–1 loss to the Cubs on June 22.

But when Orlando Cabrera questioned an official scorer in Toronto on May 4, it became outrageously overblown in the media and resulted in Cabrera suggesting that manager Ozzie Guillen was being hypocritical for telling him to "be careful" since Guillen did the same thing during his playing days. Veteran *Chicago Sun-Times* Sox beat writer Joe Cowley didn't back down from a three-minute verbal exchange with Cabrera only an hour before a game at Cleveland on May 28, and Cabrera and Guillen made their peace.

During the same week, respected conditioning director Allen Thomas and reliever Octavio Dotel got into the first of two arguments during the season. Pierzynski wasn't particularly fond of Dotel either, but the Sox were in harmony once they stepped between the white lines.

For the first five months, Quentin posted AL Most Valuable Player–type numbers: 36 home runs, 100 RBIs, and a .394 on-base percentage. His intensity caused teammates to perform a double-take, but his success was unquestioned.

Unfortunately for the White Sox, Quentin slammed his right wrist on the end of his bat in frustration after fouling off a pitch in Cleveland on September 1. Quentin had been used to hitting his fist at the end of the bat, but this time he missed. X-rays taken two days later revealed a fracture, and Quentin was lost for the final 26 games and the postseason.

Through all the setbacks and turmoil, the White Sox pulled together when a crisis reached a zenith during the season's final week.

One day after mild-mannered Javier Vazquez was caught by television cameras swearing at Pierzynski, Mark Buehrle beat Cleveland on the final day of the regular season. That victory forced the rescheduling of a makeup game against the Detroit

Tigers at U.S. Cellular Field. A Sox win would send them to a one-game playoff against the Twins; a loss would send them home for the winter.

Under soggy conditions, Ramirez's grand slam and Floyd's 17th win (on three days' rest) earned the Sox a one-game tiebreaker with their nemesis from Minnesota.

Little did anyone know that five-year-old Jake Hahn, the son of White Sox assistant GM Rick Hahn, would have a bearing in this game. Two weeks earlier, the younger Hahn told his father to call "heads" for the coin flip to determine home-field advantage in the event that both teams ended the regular season tied.

Hahn followed his son's advice, and the decision paid off after the Detroit victory.

So on a crisp night on which U.S. Cellular Field observed a "Black Out" with fans dressed in all-black attire, Danks cast a gloomy spell over a pesky Twins lineup that Guillen adored.

The Sox preserved a scoreless tie when 38-year-old Ken Griffey Jr. managed to make a running catch and one-hop throw to home plate, where Pierzynski caught the ball before he was steamrolled by Michael Cuddyer.

Pierzynski held onto the ball and showed it to Cuddyer for added emphasis to end the fifth. Danks, also throwing on short rest, allowed only two hits through eight innings but didn't have a margin for error until Thome launched a 461-foot home run in the seventh off crafty Nick Blackburn.

The White Sox's third AL Central title since 2000 wasn't complete until Anderson, a defensive standout who had replaced Griffey, made a diving catch of Alexi Casilla's fly ball to end the game.

The White Sox advanced to the AL Division Series but were overmatched by a relentless Tampa Bay team in losing the series 3–1.

"We did our best, but we ran out of gas," said Konerko, who hit two home runs in the ALDS.

LOW COST, HIGH RETURN

Arizona's re-signing of flamboyant outfielder Eric Byrnes to a three-year, $30 million contract on August 7, 2007, was supposed to spell doom for the White Sox in their attempt to re-sign right fielder Jermaine Dye, whom general manager Kenny Williams elected not to trade before the July 31 trading deadline.

The Byrnes signing, however, had a greater effect on another transaction. And it wasn't the two-year, $22 million contract Dye and the White Sox agreed to less than two weeks later that gave the franchise cost certainty and Dye some career security.

No, the Byrnes signing paved the way for Carlos Quentin's move to the White Sox.

Quentin was the Diamondbacks' second first-round pick in 2003, but his career was hampered by injuries. To make matters gloomier for Quentin, the re-signing of Byrnes, combined with the instant emergence of 2005 No. 1 overall pick Justin Upton, set Arizona's outfield for several years. Upton made the jump from Double A after Quentin was placed on the 15-day disabled list because of a right hamstring pull.

Upton instantly helped Arizona win the National League West with his speed and solidified his hold on right field after Quentin returned. With Chris Young, a former White Sox prospect, displaying a blend of power and speed in right, Quentin was expendable.

While rehabbing his hamstring at Triple-A Tucson, Quentin was watched closely by White Sox scouts Joe Butler and Gary Pellant.

They marveled at Quentin's natural power and ability to play through a tear in his left labrum that would require off-season surgery. Quentin's pain tolerance is amazing—he played his entire junior season at Stanford with a ligament tear in his right throwing elbow that required surgery immediately after signing with Arizona.

While much of the initial scrutiny at the winter meetings in Nashville surrounded the destiny of Florida slugger Miguel Cabrera, White Sox general manager Kenny Williams made a move that would quietly make skeptics forget Williams' inability to keep Cabrera from going to AL Central rival Detroit.

With outfielders Brian Anderson and Ryan Sweeney each coming off stagnant, injury-plagued years at Triple-A Charlotte, Williams was able to justify landing another young outfielder.

And with Paul Konerko signed through 2010, Williams was able to reinforce his commitment to winning now by trading Class A first baseman Chris Carter, the organization's top power-hitting prospect.

When Quentin arrived at spring training, he was a curious study to say the least. While several reporters frequently hovered around the locker of the tattooed, witty Anderson, Quentin quietly dressed one stall over.

Quentin nearly didn't get a chance to make the Opening Day roster after he was quickly shut down for a week by Williams, who noticed that Quentin was compensating for his still-healing left shoulder.

Anderson gradually worked his way out of manager Ozzie Guillen's doghouse by producing offensively and defensively and not complaining about several two-hour bus rides from Tucson to the Phoenix area.

Quentin, meanwhile, had to show the staff he was healthy and capable of producing. He demonstrated those traits while Jerry Owens, who was targeted as the White Sox's starting center fielder and leadoff batter, suffered a setback in his recovery from a groin strain he suffered in an intrasquad game two days before the start of exhibition play.

Quentin didn't start the first two games of the regular season but made a steady impact once he broke into the starting lineup. He hit safely in his first five games and impressed Guillen with his ability to settle for walks if he didn't find a pitch he liked.

He finished April with seven home runs, 21 RBIs, and a .302 batting average. His production, in light of the struggles of veterans such as Jim Thome and Paul Konerko and newcomer Nick Swisher, prompted Guillen to elevate Quentin from near the bottom of the order to the third spot as part of a mass shakeup before a May 14 game at Anaheim.

Quentin proved Guillen correct when he ripped a grand slam off Los Angeles Angels reliever Scot Shields in the eighth inning to give the White Sox a 6–1 win, a victory that ignited an eight-game winning streak.

Eleven days later, Quentin helped the Sox snap a two-game losing streak by going 3-for-3 with two home runs, including a solo shot off the Angels' John Lackey to lead off the bottom of the ninth, for a 3–2 win.

Quentin's first-half success earned him his first All-Star Game selection, as well as more attention surrounding whether he could handle the pressure of a pennant race.

"I'm prepared for anything right now," Quentin said while looking directly at the questioner. "This is what I do. This is baseball. You prepare yourself for what you are going to experience. I don't know how to say this and I want to say this in the right way. There are a lot of things in life more important than attention. So when I say I'm prepared for whatever happens in this game, I say that having experienced lows in this game like every player and you experience good things.

"I'm not going to be frightened by anything, if that's what you are saying," Quentin said, adding, "I'm going to be fine, how's that?"

Quentin's quiet personality was a contrast to the likes of Swisher and Anderson, whose lockers sandwiched Quentin's.

It's tough to pin down Quentin for an interview of more than a couple questions, as he's frequently busy preparing for an opposing pitcher or receiving treatment on his shoulder.

"He's a different human being," Guillen said. "You ask him one question and it takes him like two minutes to respond, and he gives you the right one. I think I should look in the mirror and be like him and don't say whatever's coming on my mind first.

"This kid doesn't change. You can see once in a while he has a smile on his face, but when you're on the plane he acts the same way as he does on the field, in the hotel, in the clubhouse."

Unfortunately for the White Sox, Quentin's storybook season took a big hit during a freak accident at Cleveland on September 1.

Facing Indians left-hander Cliff Lee, Quentin fouled off a pitch and slammed his arm against the top of the bat.

Quentin went on to ground into a game-ending double play that gave Lee his 20th victory.

Carlos Quentin was a revelation for the Sox in 2008 and won the Silver Slugger Award. Photo courtesy of AP Images.

Quentin, meanwhile, didn't notice something was wrong with his wrist until about 40 minutes after the game.

"It's something I've done thousands of times since I was a kid," Quentin recalled. "I had my bat in my left hand and kind of hit down on the bat head with my right hand [with a] closed fist. I hit it a little bit low and nicked my wrist.

"I finished the at-bat, and 40 minutes later I started feeling something in my wrist. I woke up the next morning, and that was that. It's something I've done a lot. Unfortunately, it hit the bone perfectly and not in a good spot."

X-rays revealed a break that halted Quentin's bid for the American League MVP Award.

But he immediately shot down a reckless report that he had suffered the injury while punching a locker in Boston the previous weekend.

"I would like to make it clear I did not punch a wall," Quentin said. "I would not do that. What did happen, it's kind of unfortunate and something that...jeez, I still have trouble believing it happened that way."

OZZIE GUILLEN

The acquisition of Ozzie Guillen was by process of elimination, as one driven White Sox scout presented his idea to chairman Jerry Reinsdorf during the 1984 season in the midst of a fifth-place finish in the American League West.

"I went to Jerry and I said, 'Look, we're not going to win with [Scott] Fletcher,'" said Jerry Krause, who went on to greater fame as the architect of the Chicago Bulls dynasty after his days as a White Sox scout were over. "'We need to get ourselves a shortstop.' We won once with Fletcher and we weren't going to win with him again. So I had an idea."

Krause scoured the organizational rosters of all the major league teams and found several clubs with prospects whose paths were blocked because of established major league shortstops ahead of them.

"No one is going to trade a guy until they have someone ahead of them," Krause recalled.

In this case, Krause discovered that Ernest Riles, a switch-hitter, was playing behind future Hall of Famer Robin Yount in Milwaukee. Jose Uribe, whose last name was Gonzalez at the time, was behind Ozzie Smith in St. Louis before he was dealt to San Francisco in a multiplayer trade for Jack Clark.

Krause also noticed that a small 20-year-old Venezuelan by the name of Ozzie Guillen played for San Diego's Triple-A affiliate in Las Vegas and was blocked by Garry Templeton.

"So I saw Ozzie and called Roland [Hemond] and said, 'Roland, I think I found the guy,'" Krause said.

The pursuit of Guillen intensified, with Krause watching him for 17 consecutive games in four different ballparks.

"I showed up to the park early every day," Krause said. "I stayed in the hotel with him. I watched him like a hawk. He always was the first one on the field. He always watched the other team take batting practice. I got nuts about him. I loved him."

This further convinced Krause to tell Reinsdorf and Hemond in August that Guillen was the player they wanted. Krause's reports supported what fellow scout and former Sox scouting director Duane Shaffer submitted earlier.

The only issue at the time was that the Padres were in the midst of a National League West pennant race and were lukewarm about trading him, especially if Templeton got hurt in the stretch drive. Krause remained hopeful that he could still land Guillen, partly based on his friendship with "Trader Jack" McKeon, San Diego's GM.

"Roland went to San Diego while the Padres were still in a pennant race," Krause said. "We talked to them, and they wanted quality pitching for a 20-year-old shortstop that basically no one had heard of."

The Padres went on to win eight of nine, prompting McKeon to tell the White Sox, "We're not going to trade the guy. We're going to win this thing and we want to keep him."

"I kept saying to Roland, 'This little shit can play. We got to do something to get him. He's a little shit, but he can play,'" Krause recalled. "I even put in the report, 'Little shit.' I figured maybe he'd hit .260 his rookie year, if that. But I thought he was the best young defensive shortstop I'd seen. He always threw guys out—he'd throw the fast guys out by a step and he'd throw the slow guys out by a step. And I thought this son of a gun knows exactly what he's doing all the time."

The White Sox headed to the winter meetings and met with McKeon, only to make no progress. Krause, determined to land Guillen, told Reinsdorf and Hemond that he had a good relationship with McKeon and asked to take another shot at landing his prized shortstop, who hit .296 and struck out only 40 times for the Las Vegas Stars.

Krause received permission, found McKeon in a hotel lobby, and talks progressed to the point where they left for McKeon's room to accelerate discussions.

The Padres initially sought left-handed pitchers before asking about LaMarr Hoyt, who slumped in 1984 after winning the AL Cy Young Award the previous year.

Krause relayed the news to Hemond, and they realized they'd need more players in return if Hoyt was going to be involved in the deal.

Krause admitted his evaluation wasn't so great when pursuing left-hander Tim Lollar, but he also sought infielder Luis Salazar.

Eventually, Krause brought a trade proposal to Reinsdorf and Hemond at about 1:00 AM and explained the only holdup was which minor leaguers to deal.

"So Reinsdorf stepped up and said, 'Let me go get [Padres president] Ballard Smith,'" Krause said. "He said, 'Give me a list of guys we don't care for if we lose them.'"

Reinsdorf woke up Smith and the deal was finished at about 4:00 AM, with the White Sox receiving Guillen, Salazar, Lollar, and pitcher Bill Long for Hoyt and minor league pitchers Todd Simmons and Kevin Kristan.

"Reinsdorf comes back to the room, looks at me and says, 'You got your boy,'" Krause said. "And he added, 'It cost us Hoyt and these minor leaguers.' I say, 'Fine, great, no problem.'"

Before the trade was announced at a news conference, Krause was approached by Hall of Fame writer Jerome Holtzman in a hallway.

"'I won't quote you, but I understand that you did a lot on this,'" Krause recalled Holtzman telling him. Krause confirmed he had some involvement, but Holtzman wanted more information on Guillen.

"I said, 'He's the closest thing to [Luis] Aparicio that I've ever seen, and he might be as good,'" Krause recalled. "'He might not hit early on, but he'll hit, eventually.' I looked at my report on him a year ago, and it was funny to look back. He hit better his rookie year than I thought he would."

Holtzman asked if he could quote Krause on the record but was denied. "'No, Jerome, you can't quote me on a guy who is as good as Aparicio. I'm not crazy,'" Krause said. "Jerome said, 'You think he's that good?'

"I said, 'Jerome, he'll be our shortstop next year and for the next 10 years afterward. This sucker is going to play.' It turned out it happened that way."

In the spring of 1985, Krause accepted an offer from Reinsdorf to become the Bulls' GM, but he was invited by Reinsdorf to meet Guillen in person.

"You call me little shit?" Guillen asked Krause, who confirmed the phrase. Krause replied, "You are a little shit. But you can play. You're going to be a hell of a player."

Krause said he told Guillen, "You can own this town some day," adding that White Sox fans loved fellow Venezuelan Aparicio and that Aparicio was their best player.

Five years later, Krause was entrenched in building a dynasty with the Bulls while Guillen quickly became one of the best defensive shortstops in baseball. But Krause found time to visit the White Sox that summer.

"I walked into the locker room, and Ozzie runs at me," Krause recalls. "'Jerry, Jerry, I got to talk to you,'" Guillen told Krause.

"No more little shit, no more little shit."

Krause was puzzled by Guillen's words.

"He takes me back to the clubhouse and there's Craig Grebeck," Krause said. The 5'11" Guillen stood next to Grebeck, who was four inches shorter, and said, "No more little shit. *He's* little shit now."

THE START OF SOMETHING BIG

Ozzie Guillen made his major league debut April 9, 1985, as the White Sox's starting shortstop and...leadoff hitter.

That's cause for pause, since Guillen wasn't known for his patience at the plate. But he went 1-for-5 in the White Sox's 4–2 win at Milwaukee and proved he could more than hold his own as a 21-year-old rookie playing for a new organization.

"It's funny," Guillen recalled 23 years later. "I was just playing baseball. I didn't follow baseball because I didn't think I was going to be in the majors any sooner. Garry Templeton was the short-stop for the Padres. I was having a good year, and then all of a sudden I wished I could play with that team one time, one year. That was in the summer of 1984."

Ozzie Guillen was a three-time All-Star and won a Gold Glove Award during his 13-year White Sox career. Photo courtesy of Getty Images.

That same summer Guillen said he saw a poster with Carlton Fisk and Tom Seaver—both with the White Sox at the time.

"I saw the poster and said, 'Look at these guys.' A couple months later, I get traded to that team," he said.

Guillen thought Templeton's knees were in bad shape and that he might stay with the Padres organization despite the knowledge that scout and former White Sox pitcher Bart Johnson had watched him play for a few days in Venezuela.

"I put in seven years with the White Sox, and Templeton was still playing for the Padres," Guillen laughed.

But when Guillen joined the White Sox for his first spring training, it was no laughing matter.

"Willie Thompson was the equipment manager, and I got to Bradenton Airport, where you got one exit, one gate," Guillen recalled. "And I come with Luis Salazar from Venezuela, and Willie was a big, funny guy. You wouldn't think a guy that big would be so nice because if I was that big, I'd never be nice to anyone. And he said, 'Where's Ozzie?'

"And Luis Salazar said, 'This is Ozzie.' And you should have seen the face on this guy, like, *What the hell, what's going on? This is Ozzie?*"

"I remember Carlton Fisk calling one of my coaches in the minor leagues, Manny Crespo. Manny told him, 'Don't worry. This kid will beat you in different ways, and you won't know what the hell is going on. He will find a way to win a game.'"

Guillen knew he had a lot to prove from the start.

"Jerry Krause told Jerry [Reinsdorf] that when he saw me for the first time, people were saying, 'What are we doing?' It was a big deal to make that trade. Even the players had questions. The players loved Fletcher, and I was the one who was going to take his spot. And they loved LaMarr and those guys."

Greg Walker concurred with Guillen's comments.

"I watched Ozzie evolve," said Walker, who was two seasons ahead of Guillen with the White Sox. "Ozzie was a street-smart kid when he first came over. We traded LaMarr Hoyt for him, and when he showed up, he weighed 140 pounds. Everyone said, 'Who is this guy?'

"I'll never forget taking ground balls the first day of spring training and taking throws from him. Nothing special. Then they hit him slow rollers and he fielded them bare-handed and I'd never seen that before. It was obvious he had a special knack and was a street-smart baseball player. We saw that from the first day."

Finally, the scrutiny came to a head.

"I remember Pudge making comments, and Tony La Russa telling Pudge to 'Shut the [bleep] up and catch. That's not your business. You're just a catcher.' I think Tony did it to make me comfortable," Guillen recalled.

Guillen said jumping into a tough situation helped him persevere.

"I know the competition was going to be tough because we had Scott Fletcher here, and he was playing every day," said Guillen. "But when you get to an organization, you don't know how long you're going to be there. And the only thing you do is play hard, have some respect, represent the organization the right way. Then you take a chance."

Guillen earned American League Rookie of the Year honors by batting .273 and providing exceptional defense. In the process, he started to become a stable leader by learning from several of his more seasoned teammates.

"I think what made me stay that long with the White Sox [as a player] were the teammates I grew up with," Guillen said. "I love and care about this organization. When I came here, I was the only kid on the team besides Tim Hulett. Then you see Pudge and Baines and Greg Walker and Floyd Bannister and Seaver and Richard Dotson, and you see guys here for a while and being raised by Tony La Russa and all those guys.

"A lot of people thought I grew up with this organization. A lot of people think I'm a White Sox from the farm. It's something I appreciate because it means a lot to me."

The traits Guillen learned from his teammates included honesty, leadership, and friendship.

"I got the leadership from Pudge, the honesty from Baines and Walker," Guillen said. "I got the friendship from Bainesy. I was lucky to grow up in that era—very, very lucky. A lot of people say that to kiss peoples' [asses]. I was very lucky. They taught me to be a gamer. They taught me to play every day. They taught me there's nothing bigger than the game.

"Herm Schneider taught me how to handle pain on the field. You see guys on the field with headaches, and they cannot even play. But I don't think you're going to see that anymore. I don't think you're going to see a real leader in baseball anymore because money is involved, friendships are involved."

Guillen remembered one valuable lesson learned from Tom Seaver at Yankee Stadium.

"I hit a line drive in New York, and Dave Winfield made the play, and I was throwing helmets and balls all over the place, and Tom Seaver didn't like it," Guillen said. "And he let me know as soon as I walked to the dugout. It was on. And I never thought or took it as he hated me or didn't like me. He was just teaching me to be a professional.

"Now when you do that, now you're an ass, not a good teammate. I just learned from that, and I learned to be a good leader. I was a leader hitting .225, .250, .270. I wasn't the best player on the team, but I was the best one to represent the club."

Guillen's achievements (three All-Star selections, a 1990 Gold Glove Award for his defense) were modest, but his ability to pass along the traits he

Ozzie Guillen played 13 years on the South Side after being acquired from the Padres in 1984.

learned from his veteran teammates made him an ideal leader when young talent like Robin Ventura, Frank Thomas, and Alex Fernandez reached the majors.

"I don't say I was 'the guy, the god' around them," Guillen said. "When they got here, I had my few years, and I was the leader on the club. They knew right away—Frank, a Hall of Famer. Robin, unbelievable career. Fernandez, unbelievable career. I grew up around horse[bleep] players, too.

"But one thing about growing up here, when you see a [former teammate], and a good percentage of the guys see you and hug you, it's just awesome. And I grew up in two eras. I grew up in the old school, the 1983 bull[bleep], and the new era that's coming out, the White Sox we remember now."

KNEE-JING A CHALLENGE

In 1992, Guillen was coming off two consecutive All-Star years and had played in 149 games or more in seven consecutive seasons.

That came to an end on April 21, when Guillen's knee collided with the shoulder of left fielder Tim Raines, causing ligament tears in Guillen's knee that ended his season after only 12 games.

"I was in the hospital, and it was a Catholic hospital because there were a lot of nuns," Guillen said. "And Robin and Joey [Cora] showed up with a lot of beers, and they threw a party in my room. And all of a sudden, the next day they wanted to kick me out of the hospital. That's the kind of teammates I grew up with. Now teammates just call you and ask, 'How are you doing?' Those guys drove to the hospital to support me."

After getting by on natural talent, Guillen had to motivate himself to rehabilitate his knee and received some stern words from trainer Herm Schneider.

"As soon as I started working out, Hermie told me I was lazy," Guillen recalled. "I don't like to work out. I was natural. I wasn't spending time in a weight room or in the off-season getting ready to play. God gave me natural talent. And Hermie said, 'This is the first time you have to work. You don't work, you'll never play baseball again.'

"God put stuff in my way to see how much I loved baseball. You look around and I said, 'All right.' A lot of people thought I never was going to come back. I wasn't the guy who was going to put a lot of hours and time to work out, but I did."

Guillen bounced back in 1993, hitting .280 and .288 in successive seasons. Although his speed and range diminished, he remained the White Sox's shortstop through the 1997 season before he was replaced by Mike Caruso.

"What was big at that point [after the surgery] was that he still was one of the better shortstops in the league, and he had to work hard to maintain that level of excellence," Ventura recalled. "Guys like Ripken were dominating the position, but Ozzie was still a tough out."

The injury might have been a blessing in disguise for his future, Walker hinted.

"As Ozzie's career went on, he became more of a student of the game, a more disciplined player, and he probably understood early on he wanted to stay in this game and be a manager," Walker said.

And those traits helped Guillen win 2005 American League Manager of the Year honors from the Baseball Writers Association of America by directing the White Sox to 99 victories and letting his starting pitchers work deep into games. Under Guillen, the Sox were 61–33 in games decided by two runs or less, including a 34–13 mark against the AL Central in those games.

HANGING-OVER

Three months after winning the World Series, Guillen revealed that he was hung over during his interview for the White Sox's job.

Guillen divulged this to HBO's James Brown in an episode of *Real Sports with Bryant Gumbel*, telling Brown that he partied with Florida catcher Ivan "Pudge" Rodriguez after winning the 2003 World Series with Florida, where Guillen served as a third-base coach under Jack McKeon.

GM Kenny Williams hired former teammate Ozzie Guillen in 2003, making Guillen the 37ᵗʰ manager in team history. Photo courtesy of AP Images.

Brown asked Guillen if he rehearsed his answers prior to the interview, conducted at a restaurant located west of Chicago.

"No, I was hung over," Guillen replied.

Said Brown, "You did what?" Guillen repeated his answer, which Brown questioned.

"Just because, we just won the World Series. I was at Pudge Rodriguez's house, and we had a party all night to celebrate the World Series," Guillen said.

OZZIE TAKES ON THE WORLD

With few exceptions, Guillen has stated he's never thrown the first verbal punch in his numerous battles in the media. But he's one of the last guys in baseball to back down from any squabble, no matter how small. To Guillen, protecting his players and the White Sox organization is as important as protecting his wife and three sons.

Guillen vs. Magglio Ordonez

A sleepy Thursday morning at Comerica Park in 2005 turned volcanic after Guillen learned that former White Sox slugger and fellow Venezuelan Magglio Ordonez had called him an "enemy."

"He's a piece of [bleep]," Guillen said after being told that Ordonez alleged his former manager got involved in negotiations that eventually pushed Ordonez to Detroit after the 2004 season.

"He's a [bleep], that's what he is," Guillen continued. "He's another Venezuelan [bleep]. [Bleep] him. He has an enemy. Now he has a big one. He knows I can [bleep] him a lot of different ways. He better shut the [bleep] up and play for the Detroit Tigers."

Ordonez wasn't playing at the time because of a sports hernia, but calmly expressed the lack of camaraderie between himself and Guillen from the time they played together briefly in 1997 and during Guillen's first year as manager in 2004.

"We never clicked, even when we played together," Ordonez said. "I don't consider him my friend. I have nothing to say. I don't want to see him or talk to him. He's my enemy. If he comes to me and wants to apologize, I wouldn't accept it."

That suggestion infuriated Guillen.

"Why do I have to apologize to him?" Guillen barked. "Who the [bleep] is Magglio Ordonez? Why ever talk about me? He doesn't do [bleep] for me. But if he thinks I'm his enemy, he has a big enemy. He knows me."

Guillen added later, "I think Magglio is playing with fire. I'm not afraid of him. I have nothing to apologize [for]. I have nothing to do with Magglio wearing the Detroit Tigers uniform. Every time when he played for me, he played good. But if he thinks I'm his enemy or I have something against him, it's up to him."

Guillen said he went to general manager Ron Schueler to endorse Ordonez as a player in 1997.

"I'm not here to make friends," Guillen said. "I'm here to win games. I have a lot of friends. If Magglio doesn't want to be my friend, I don't have to drink with him. A couple people asked me about it, and I was nice about his injury and [bleep]. I don't give a [bleep] what he does for the rest of his life. He [bleeped] with the wrong guy."

Guillen and Ordonez made their peace in the off-season.

Guillen vs. Alex Rodriguez

One day before the White Sox opened defense of their 2005 World Series title, a *Sports Illustrated* story on Guillen hit the newsstands and invited more scrutiny.

In particular, it was Guillen's harsh comments toward New York Yankees superstar Alex Rodriguez that caused the most attention.

"Alex was kissing Latino people's asses," Guillen said. "He knew he wasn't going to play for the Dominicans [in the World Baseball Classic]; he's not a Dominican!"

Guillen added later, "I hate hypocrites. He's full of [bleep]. The Dominican team doesn't need his ass. It's the same with [Nomar] Garciaparra playing for Mexico. Garciaparra only knows Cancun because he went to visit."

The next day, Guillen sat on a picnic bench under cloudy skies outside the Sox's major league clubhouse in Tucson, Arizona, and issued an apology to Rodriguez, his family, his fans, the Yankees organization, and the White Sox.

"I learned a lesson," Guillen said. "I never took a first shot at anybody in my life and now I feel like I took the first shot. I feel embarrassed, I feel guilty. I wish I had not said it the way it sounds or the way I said it."

Guillen vs. Kelvim Escobar

Showing no favoritism toward his countrymen, Guillen called out Los Angeles Angels pitcher Kelvim Escobar for hitting catcher A.J. Pierzynski with two out and nobody on in the second inning of an April 29, 2006, game, less than one year after Pierzynski wisely ran to first after a controversial dropped third strike that helped the Sox seize a victory in Game 2 of the American League Championship Series.

"Who gives a [bleep] what happened last year?" Guillen snapped. "And if Escobar is going to hit somebody, he should hit

CROSSTOWN CHEAP SHOT

After getting barbecued by his own players, fans, and a reporter during a miserable 2004 season in San Francisco, catcher A.J. Pierzynski became an instant hit with the White Sox because of his durability, clutch hitting, and intangibles that helped his team win.

That said, Pierzynski can occasionally rub even his White Sox teammates the wrong way. One of the most common scenes in baseball is the starting pitcher, the starting catcher, and the pitching coach walking from the bullpen to the dugout before the start of a game.

But one night after hitting a game-winning home run against Cleveland on July 2, 2008, Pierzynski left the bullpen well ahead of pitcher Javier Vazquez and got a standing ovation while walking to the dugout. That didn't go unnoticed by several teammates who rolled their eyes.

Nevertheless, Pierzynski had the full support of his teammates after he was victimized by a sucker punch in 2006 in a game against the rival Cubs.

On a warm Saturday afternoon on May 20, Pierzynski tagged up from third base and slammed into Cubs catcher Michael Barrett, who was trying to block home plate without possessing the ball.

Pierzynski retreated to tag home plate with his hand, then started to pick up his helmet, which was sitting near Barrett.

Barrett grabbed Pierzynski and paused before smacking him in the face without provocation. Scott Podsednik immediately tackled Barrett while Brian Anderson, the batter who hit the sacrifice fly, took a few swings at the Cubs' John Mabry as both teams poured out of their dugouts.

Barrett admitted his wrongdoing immediately after the incident and apologized personally to Pierzynski before the Sox-Cubs rematch one month later at Wrigley. The incident actually ignited a slogan—"Punch A.J."—that successfully encouraged fans to select Pierzynski for the final spot on the 2006 American League All-Star team.

But in one of the most puzzling moves by Bob Watson, Major League Baseball's vice president of on-field activities, Pierzynski was fined $2,000 for his conduct during the incident. Pierzynski got his fine reduced to $250, but expressed his displeasure with what he perceived as Watson's reasoning.

"I understand what I had to pay," Pierzynski said. "But at the same time, the thing that bothered me was that during the hearing, Bob Watson said I was fined for things that happened the next day. For trying to bunt, for trying to slide too hard to break up a double play the next day. That was the thing that bothered me more than anything during the appeal on the phone. He said I was fined for the way I played."

himself. A.J. had nothing to do with the dumbass play they make. [It was catcher] Josh Paul and him. Those are two dumb [bleeping] plays they make, and now all of a sudden they're blaming it on A.J. You have to be dumb enough to blame it on somebody when you screw it up. That's my point. That's a low-ass way to play baseball."

Guillen went on to suggest that Southern California fans should remember Escobar's inability to retrieve the dropped third strike in the same manner that New England fans barbecued Boston first baseman Bill Buckner for allowing a grounder to go under his glove in Game 6 of the 1986 World Series.

"Blame yourself," Guillen continued. "And now you're talking like you're going to hit somebody with no reason. You can get somebody hurt with no reason. That thing bugs me, because people in this league think I'm a [bleeping] headhunter."

Guillen vs. Rich Hill

Hill threw some gas on the fire stemming from a fight-marred 7–0 loss to the White Sox on May 20, 2006, in which the Cubs left-hander was tagged for seven runs on five hits and five walks in four innings.

After learning that Hill had called Pierzynski, who was sucker-punched by Cubs catcher Michael Barrett, "gutless" and "pathetic," Guillen threw some verbal jabs at Hill.

"Tell that Triple-A [bleep] to shut the [bleep] up," Guillen said. "Tell him to start throwing some strikes or he's going to get Dusty [Baker] fired."

Hill was optioned the next day, bringing a smile to Guillen's face.

Guillen vs. Brandon McCarthy

McCarthy became a rookie hero in 2005 by winning games at Texas and at Boston (beating Curt Schilling), but was dealt after the 2006 season to the Rangers for pitchers John Danks and Nick Masset.

After learning that McCarthy felt more comfortable in the Rangers' spring-training clubhouse because he had more in common with his younger teammates, Guillen defended his players at McCarthy's expense.

Guillen even revealed that he had longtime friends in Chicago tell him that McCarthy was seen out late at bars with teammate and friend Brian Anderson.

"I don't want to talk about Mac because he made a couple of comments—I really hate him," Guillen said. "I don't like the comments he made about our clubhouse, about our players, about 'negative' people here. There's one thing about Ozzie Guillen: Ozzie Guillen is never negative.

"You played with us 162 games and all of a sudden you leave and say you don't have a friend in the clubhouse? Only Brian Anderson? Well, he picked the wrong guy to be friends with. People forgot that Brandon McCarthy got caught a couple of times out at night. I called him into my office and said, 'You been hanging around the city a lot, huh?' I said, 'I don't have a spy on you, but I know a lot of people in the bars in Chicago. I've been here for 20 years, and they will tell me everything.'"

Guillen added, "He forgot he lost a couple of games for us. He lost at least five of the 72. We might be in the playoffs without him."

Ozzie Guillen has had numerous run-ins with reporters, managers, and even his own players, including former Sox pitcher Brandon McCarthy.
Photo courtesy of AP Images.

Guillen vs. Jim Edmonds

This was one-sided, as Edmonds merely hit two home runs in one inning in the Cubs' 11–7 win over the White Sox at Wrigley Field on June 21, 2008.

But Guillen wasn't about to marvel over Edmonds' achievement.

"I don't want to promote the guy who is just hitting [.238] and [stuff]," Guillen said in a cramped visiting manager's office. "He just had a good day. Good for them. I think I'd rather have him out there than [Alfonso] Soriano.

"Believe me, I do. Jim is a veteran player who knows what he's doing. He swings the bat well and they got him because someone got hurt or whatever the reason is. Hopefully he doesn't have another game like that against us.

"Jim is Jim. Jim is not going to scare me. I will pitch to him another time. He just hit a couple home runs. Good for him."

Guillen vs. His Hitters

After watching his batters go 2-for-14 with runners in scoring position in a 4–3 loss at Tampa Bay on June 1, 2008, Guillen blasted his offense and called out some of his staff members.

"Just be ready because I expect movement," Guillen said before rushing to catch a flight to Miami for an off-day. "I expect [general manager] Kenny Williams to do something Tuesday, and if we don't do anything Tuesday, there are going to be a lot of lineup changes. That's all I'm going to say about the offense. It can be me. It can be [hitting coach] Greg Walker. It can be the players. It could be anybody. I'm sick and tired to watch this thing for a year and a half. I'm not protecting anybody anymore. [Bleep] it. If they can't get it done, Kenny should find someone to get it done. That's it."

"Another bad game," Guillen added later. "If we think we are going to win with the offense we have, we are full of [bleep]. I'm just being honest. I expect better from them, if they are in the lineup."

After being informed of Guillen's comments, Williams initially took exception.

"It's just not a good idea to throw your boss under the bus, especially when that boss has had your back as much as I have had his," Williams wrote in an e-mail. "I expect this team, if the leadership remains positive and the players stick together and continue to play hard, it will be a fun summer.

"The offense will begin to produce when collectively they say, the hell with all the theories, stay loose, pick the pitch you want to hit and hit it hard. It will be nice to see them lighten up and have some fun."

Two days later, Williams met with Guillen, and the manager said he felt bad about putting his GM on the spot, especially after having his contract extended to 2012 during the end of a 90-loss season in 1997. 2007

At any rate, the Sox embarked on a seven-game winning streak after Guillen's explosion.

Guillen vs. C.J. Wilson

As a fierce protector of his veterans, Guillen didn't like the way Texas' left-handed reliever was barking at veteran Jim Thome after striking him out during the ninth inning of a miserable 12–11 loss in searing heat on July 13, 2008.

"Wait until you're somebody in baseball, and then do whatever you want to do," Guillen said of Wilson.

Wilson told the *Dallas Morning News* that "I didn't have good stuff, and then I got angry when Ozzie Guillen started yelling at me, and I just took it to another level."

Guillen said Wilson was "acting like he was the first ever to strike out Jim Thome. Jim Thome has 4,000 strikeouts."

"Mariano Rivera never showed anyone up," Guillen said. "You got your own style, but you don't show up another team. That's when I started screaming. I think he should read my quote about whoever pitched in that game should be embarrassed, because when you bring in the closer with a [four]-run lead, and you almost blew it, and you're acting like you're [Lee] Smith or Goose Gossage. And that's embarrassing when you're cocky and got [nothing]."

Ten days after the incident, the White Sox got revenge when Carlos Quentin hit a three-run home run off Wilson to cap a 10–8 comeback win.

"Always out there are the baseball gods," Guillen said. "Be careful what you do and what you say in this game because [they're] going to get you back."

Guillen vs. Buck Showalter

Talk about polar opposites. While Guillen played 16 seasons and was a major league coach for three seasons before taking over the White Sox's managing duties, Showalter was a .294 hitter in seven minor league seasons in the New York Yankees system before working his way to a managerial career and helping build contenders with the Yankees and the expansion Arizona Diamondbacks shortly before they became world champions.

So it was supposed to be a simple inquiry when Guillen asked umpires why Texas pitching instructor John Wetteland was allowed to coach first base in place of suspended Rangers coach Steve Smith during a 7–3 win in Arlington on September 9, 2004.

But in Showalter's postgame press conference, he raised the issue of why Guillen would ask about the move.

"I guess he didn't know you could carry seven coaches in September or an extra coach in September," Showalter said.

Guillen, finishing his first year as manager, took that as an insult and bombarded Showalter with insults of his own.

"When the 'best manager' in the history of baseball talks about you, that means you're on somebody's mind," Guillen said. "And when you're beating the crap out of the best manager in baseball, and we beat the [bleep] out of them, it makes me feel a lot better.

"To compete against the guy [Showalter] that invented baseball, and beat him, that's something you should feel good about as a rookie manager."

That was just the start, as Guillen said that Showalter's tendency to keep one hand in his back pocket was "so he doesn't lose the key to baseball that he keeps there when he runs on the field."

Then it became even more personal to Guillen.

"[Showalter] never even smelled a jock in the big leagues. He didn't even know how the clubhouse in the big leagues was when he got his first job.... 'Mr. Baseball' never even got a hit in Triple A. He was a backup catcher or a first baseman all his career. Now all of the sudden he's the best ever in baseball.

"It's too bad I didn't have to go to the minor leagues to get this job like he did. I was coaching straight up in the big leagues. I was a big-league coach and I went straight to big-league manager. Ozzie Guillen had to do something to take those steps. I only played two, three years in the minor leagues and played 13 years with the same team.

"There are so many different things he might be jealous [of]. I was a better player than him, I've got more money than him, and I'm better looking than him."

Guillen vs. Mariano Duncan

Guillen became the first Latin manager to win a World Series, and Duncan called Guillen a "hero" in Duncan's native Dominican Republic and a "smart guy."

But Duncan, a coach with the Los Angeles Dodgers at the time, believed that Guillen went too far in his outspokenness and wondered if his candid comments could hurt Latinos' chances for advancement in Major League Baseball.

"Think before you talk, or you can really hurt yourself and hurt a lot of other people," Duncan told the *Los Angeles Times* in a June 25, 2006, interview.

"He's opened so many doors to Latino coaches. Now he's in a position where people are listening to him. But he's throwing everything away by the way he's behaving."

Duncan went on to claim that Guillen embarrassed every Latino player, coach, and front-office person.

Guillen didn't seem impressed.

"It was a little bit too big for him to be talking about it," Guillen said. "Like I say, when you don't have anything to say, don't make any comments. When Mariano made that comment, it was like, 'Who are you?' Come on. You talk about somebody like Tony Fernandez or Davey Concepcion or Roberto Alomar. But Mariano Duncan, that's the last guy I care about what he says.

"If my job is going to close a lot of Latino people's jobs, we're going to have a lot of jobs open. Because my job is going to be the best I can for all Latin American people and I'm going to do what I can to make Latin American people feel proud. Not because you say one thing to one guy. That makes me laugh."

Guillen vs. Hunter Wendelstedt

It was supposed to be a simple ejection, with Guillen getting tossed for arguing a stolen-base call. Guillen was assessed a two-game suspension and an undisclosed fine for allegedly spitting tobacco juice on Hunter Wendelstedt.

But Guillen took matters further and alleged that Wendelstedt lied in his report to Major League Baseball officials, calling him a liar and telling him, "You're not even a pimple on your daddy's ass." Wendelstedt is the son of former MLB umpire Harry Wendelstedt.

Speaking about the incident cost Guillen an additional two games and an additional fine.

Guillen vs. Phil Cuzzi

With the Sox 13 games out of first place at the July 31, 2007, trading deadline, Guillen didn't lose his fire.

In fact, Guillen was upset when home-plate umpire Phil Cuzzi ruled that Derek Jeter checked his swing on a pitch in the first inning during a game against the Yankees.

A quick exchanged occurred, with Cuzzi tossing Guillen, who was standing in the dugout at the time of the ejection.

"If I say what I feel, I will be suspended and this guy [Cuzzi] will keep umpiring and keep [bleeping] people," Guillen said. "You look at games, and [Cuzzi] is in the middle of something.... I remember they suspended me for four days and sent me to anger management. Well, I hope the league watched this game and saw how this man was reacting to me and the player and take a real look at it and see what they can do about it.

"From 1985 to now, I don't see any umpire [disrespect] players and managers the way that guy does. That's something you don't tolerate as a manager. I see this guy do it over and over. It's time for someone to step it up.... If they're willing to fine me for what I say, I'm willing to pay that money because I called him a lot of things I'm not supposed to say."

Following another loss the next night, Guillen climbed out of a sport utility vehicle driven by New York Yankees outfielder and fellow Venezuelan Bobby Abreu, raised his arms, and yelled, "I'm baseball's bitch!" at the intersection of Madison and 39th at approximately midnight.

Guillen vs. Phil Cuzzi, Part II

A sellout crowd for the 2008 home opener on April 7 saw Guillen get tossed by Cuzzi following a Paul Konerko strikeout.

Two days later, Guillen again expressed his feelings toward Cuzzi.

"He doesn't like me, I don't like him," Guillen said. "One reason is, if you don't like me as a man and what I do, I can respect that. But if you don't like me and you're going to take it out on my players, you're wrong. That's unprofessional. I just let him know I don't like him the first day I see him, and I think he feels the same way about me. And we have to move on."

Cuzzi, however, said he had no personal problems with Guillen, who was nevertheless fined.

Guillen vs. the Media

Mounted on a bulletin board outside of Guillen's office is a *Chicago Sun-Times* column praising the White Sox's hiring of Guillen in November 2003. It reads "Wave Him Home: Guillen Right Choice for Sox."

The author of the column is Jay Mariotti, who later dubbed Guillen the "Blizzard of Oz" for the manager's outspokenness, a practice that Mariotti frequently questioned.

Guillen's ensuing hatred began to swell during the 2006 season and reached a zenith entering a series with St. Louis, one week after Mariotti criticized Guillen's antics toward rookie pitcher Sean Tracey. After Texas' Vicente Padilla hit A.J. Pierzynski with a pitch, Guillen chewed out Tracey for not retaliating against Hank Blalock. Guillen yelled in the dugout and spiked a bottle of water because of his pitcher's lack of emotion.

Toward the end of a 20-minute pregame session with reporters, Guillen embarked on a profanity-laced tirade toward Mariotti.

"He's not going to run me out of town," Guillen said. "Tell Mariotti he can kiss my ass. He's going to lose his job before I lose mine. I guarantee that. Because I plug it in every day to [bleeping] murder these mother[bleepers], to make sure I make him miserable. He thinks that talking [bleep] in the papers is going to get me fired? [Bleep] him, [bleep] him and all his people around him. I leave this [bleeping] town when I want to leave, when I've had enough, or maybe next week. Maybe in [bleeping] 20 years, mother[bleeper], but I'm going to be here for a little while. Now he's [bleeping] to get Dusty [Baker] out of there and put [bleeping] guys in the goddamn radio show."

Then came one of Guillen's biggest verbal blunders.

"What a piece of [bleep] he is, [bleeping] fag. He is a stupid [bleeping] idiot."

Guillen was zapped with a $20,000 fine and ordered to attend sensitivity classes.

"I don't regret what I say about Jay," Guillen said. "I regret what I say about the [gay] community."

Guillen vs. Mike North

En route to Wrigley Field shortly before 9:00 AM for the first game of the intercity series with the Cubs in 2007, Guillen listened to popular radio talk-show host and White Sox fan Mike North tell catcher A.J. Pierzynski that he should be starting the first game of the series instead of Toby Hall, who was recently activated.

Guillen placed a call to the show and didn't approve of North making out the lineup.

"Oh, shut the [bleep] up," Guillen snapped. "I know you like A.J. but there's no reason for you to make lineups and [bleep]. I don't care what A.J. thinks. I make the best lineup. I want to find out what Toby Hall can do for this ballclub, find out right away how we are going to use him. I never said A.J. was in a platoon. Believe me, I'm tired of you guys and this bull[bleep] every goddamn day."

North, immediately aware that the profanity violated FCC rules, interjected.

"Hey, Ozzie, clean up your mouth," he said. "Clean up your damn mouth when you're talking on the radio and talking to me. Have a little respect, all right? Don't go talking to me like you're talking down to somebody."

North, to his credit, showed up about 90 minutes later to the visitor's clubhouse and settled his differences with Guillen.

An edited version of the radio exchange was played in the clubhouse, with pitcher Mark Buehrle subtly turning up the volume.

A TORNADO IN TORONTO

While in the midst of a six-game losing streak, an unidentified member of the White Sox traveling party tried to provide some amusement early Sunday morning in the visitor's clubhouse at the Rogers Centre in Toronto on May 4, 2008.

Players were greeted by two female blow-up dolls sitting on top of a recliner with the players' bats below them. The attempt to help the hitters break out of their slumps was accompanied by signs that supported the Sox.

"Well, whoever did it spent a lot of money," Guillen chuckled. "That's the type of guys we have. The clubhouse has been quiet the last couple days and I don't like to see that. We have to stay at the same level of enthusiasm, no matter what happens. Because you worry about the game during the game. Before and after, you can't do anything about it. I know it's not easy to enjoy yourself when you're losing, but I expect the guys to stay with the same attitude no matter the results of the game."

But when a reporter joked about the possibility of the Sox promoting Class-A outfielder John Shelby Jr., who hit three home runs in a game the previous night, Guillen took the time to verbally chastise the Chicago media and fans for not displaying enough faith in the Sox's struggling lineup.

"Right now everyone in Chicago is making lineups, 'Call up this guy, call up that guy,'" Guillen said. "If we had 50 people allowed on the roster we could do that. That's what ticks me off about Chicago fans and Chicago media—they forget pretty quick. A couple of days ago we were the [bleeping] best [stuff] in town, now we're [bleep]."

Why?

"Because maybe the manager is an [bleep]," Guillen replied.

Guillen elaborated on the fact that the crosstown Cubs, who haven't won a World Series since 1908, get a free pass.

"We won it a couple years ago, and we're horse[bleep]. The Cubs haven't won in 120 years and they're the [bleeping] best," Guillen said. "[Bleep] it, we're good. [Bleep] everybody. We're horse[bleep] and we're going to be horse[bleep] the rest of our lives, no matter how many World Series we win. We are the bitch of Chicago. We're the Chicago bitch. We have the worst owner— the guy's got seven [bleeping] rings, and he's the [bleeping] horse[bleep] owner."

That was just a warm-up act.

"How about the Cubs celebrating that Lee Elia bull[bleep]?" Guillen continued. "How many times I curse people out, I will make a lot of money with my [stuff]. I have to keep going because in the future Ozzie will need money and I can say, 'Here, give me money, here's the 10-year anniversary of the time I called [Jay] Mariotti stuff and the time I went on the radio and cursed out Mike North last year.' Yeah, we have to celebrate all that [stuff], too. But I won't be around for 10 years, believe me.

"People are panicking. Did we play a real bad week? Yes, we did, we stunk. But it wasn't too long ago that we were 'the biggest surprise in baseball, wow, look at the White Sox.' All of a sudden, there we go, back to normal. We have to deal with it, [bleep] it. As long as the 25 guys out there believe we can do it, everyone else, hey..."

CHAIRMAN OF THE FAMILY

Jerry Reinsdorf grew up in Brooklyn as a fan of the Dodgers and attended the same high school as Oakland Raiders owner Al Davis.

Those roots have helped him guide the White Sox since he and Eddie Einhorn bought a controlling interest from Bill Veeck after the 1980 season.

From employees to players, there's a strong sense of loyalty that has created a lifelong bond on the South Side.

"He's got a system," said hitting coach Greg Walker, who came back to the organization in 2000. "I know he's too smart not to have a core belief in why he does what he does. You'd have to ask him. I don't know if he'd tell you. It would be an interesting discussion. He believes in people and lets you work. As long as you hold up your end of the bargain, he's an extremely loyal man."

Since taking over the NBA's Bulls and the White Sox in the early 1980s, Reinsdorf has overseen seven championships in Chicago. The White Sox's 2005 World Series title brought tremendous relief to Sox fans as well as a great sense of satisfaction and civic pride for Reinsdorf.

"Jerry is the glue," Walker continued. "All of us have been friends and teammates. We love the White Sox and the city of Chicago, but the one guy who makes us feel like part of the family is Jerry. Here is a guy who has had a lot of great players...but for some reason, he let me know he wanted me to be a part of his family forever. That's a special feeling.

"He's so well respected in the game and all of his ideas, he's been right a big majority of the time. A lot of people think he's the smartest man in baseball. Here's this brilliant man who chose a .260 hitter, couldn't run and couldn't throw, to be a part of his family."

Walker appreciates that Reinsdorf looked after him and his family after he suffered a seizure during the 1988 season, a move that Walker sensed would have been ignored by most owners.

A similar situation occurred during the 1992 season, when shortstop Ozzie Guillen was on the operating table with three badly damaged ligaments that could have affected his value in the free-agent market.

"Jerry told me on the phone, 'Tell Ozzie I'm picking up his option [for 1993],'" trainer Herm Schneider recalled. "Not many people would do that. You don't know if the guy is coming back, especially since he's a shortstop and the way you tried to come back from ACL [anterior cruciate ligament] and MCL [medial collateral ligament] injuries back then. They have better ways of [rehabbing it] now. But kudos to Jerry."

Some of Reinsdorf's biggest battles have involved former stars that have either made peace with him or have returned to the organization.

"Jerry is a good man," said slugger Frank Thomas, who appreciated Reinsdorf making a special visit to see him when Thomas visited U.S. Cellular Field with Toronto in 2007. "Jerry is misunderstood by a lot of people. Deep down, he has a good heart. But one thing, he runs a strong business. He's attached to a lot of people and he gets attached to a lot of people. But overall, he's really a good person deep down and wants to be family and friends with everyone, especially with guys who have been there a long time. He's a very loyal guy.

"He treated me wonderful during the time I was there. Breaking up was tough, but that's hard with any relationship that lasts 16 years. I'm not going to be there. But deep down, he's had a good heart. He's always had a good heart. That's not going to change."

Jerry Reinsdorf has tried to foster a family atmosphere within the White Sox organization since buying the team in 1981.

Even as the acrimony heated up during the players' strike in 1994, vocal star pitcher Jack McDowell knew Reinsdorf had to take care of his short-range and long-range interests.

"All the contract squabbles, they had a lot to do with my health, projected health, and all that kind of stuff," said McDowell, who has received rave reviews as a fill-in announcer. "I had confidence in myself. But I'm sure, looking back, they weren't too happy to have a guy with an arthritic hip that they have to deal with every year, not realizing if that was ever going to go, and I realize that end of it. And I think they realize my end of it, too."

With a competitive team that has increased its player payroll by more than 50 percent since 2005 and has enjoyed stable attendance at an upgraded U.S. Cellular Field, the controversies that Reinsdorf and vice chairman Eddie Einhorn encountered after purchasing the team from Bill Veeck seem like a lifetime ago.

Yet, the resolution of several incidents defined the current state of the organization.

BROADCASTING BUFFOONERY

Reinsdorf and Einhorn (who doesn't get enough credit for the popularity and exposure of college basketball dating back to his company's televising of the UCLA-Houston basketball game in 1968) took over the White Sox when legendary broadcaster Harry Caray and color analyst Jimmy Piersall were in their heyday.

In his book, *The Truth Hurts*, Piersall described how he and Caray "first-guessed," in which they would describe an upcoming situation and suggest what manager Tony La Russa should do. Piersall believed that this was no different from what paying customers do.

But after explaining this to Reinsdorf in a meeting, Piersall said he was told to stop.

Piersall also found himself in hot water for his comments about players' spouses.

"I think each ballclub should have clinics for wives once a week on baseball, because I really don't think they know what the game of baseball really is," Piersall said on Mike Royko's show at the famous Billy Goat Tavern. "Oh, they were just horny broads that wanted to get married, and they wanted a little money, a little security, and they wanted a big, strong ballplayer."

Piersall was suspended with pay for the rest of the 1981 season. His spat with former beat writer Rob Gallas (who went on

Harry Caray and Jimmy Piersall were a popular tandem in the White Sox broadcasting booth from 1977 to 1981.

to join the team's front office) caused venerable coach Art Kusnyer to restrain him, and he was later confronted by manager Tony La Russa and coaches Jim Leyland and Charlie Lau at a studio.

Caray, fed up with Reinsdorf and Einhorn and their handling of Piersall, left for the crosstown Cubs after the 1981 season. Caray's destiny was sealed when the Sox elected to televise their games on SportsVision, a cable channel that would provide games of the Sox, Bulls, Blackhawks, and Sting to local paying subscribers. The pay channel prevented fans from watching several White Sox games for free and thereby limited Caray's exposure.

After 11 years, Caray's stunning move to the rival Cubs and WGN-TV sent the Cubs' nationwide popularity through the roof as WGN swelled to become a superstation.

The final straw for Piersall came at the start of the 1983 season, when Piersall ripped La Russa for starting rookie Greg Walker over Mike Squires and Tom Paciorek over Ron Kittle.

Piersall was fired, and the Sox went on to win the American League West.

FROM COMISKEY PARK TO U.S. CELLULAR FIELD

When Reinsdorf and Einhorn took over the White Sox, they also took over a ballpark in its eighth decade.

More than $29 million was poured into improving Comiskey Park, but that was just postponing the inevitable. A push to build a ballpark in the west suburb of Addison was rejected by local voters in 1986.

With no current options, the White Sox took note that an indoor stadium was being built in St. Petersburg, Florida. That provided White Sox ownership with leverage if a new park wasn't built in Chicago.

The White Sox played hardball in 1988 by stating their intent to move to Florida unless Illinois politicians agreed to finance a new stadium at the end of the government session on June 30. The White Sox even signed a 15-year lease to play at the domed park in Florida contingent upon them not getting approval for a new park in Chicago.

Illinois governor Jim Thompson, meanwhile, was intent on keeping the Sox in Chicago despite some fierce opposition. Facing a midnight deadline, Thompson worked the Illinois House and Senate and beat the deadline—with some help.

House speaker Michael Madigan stopped the clock at 11:59 PM, buying Thompson extra time to get the necessary votes to pass a measure to fund a new stadium across the street from the old Comiskey Park.

Construction at the new Comiskey Park started in May 1989 and was completed in time for the 1991 season. It was built at a cost of $137 million to taxpayers, although the White Sox have contributed to the $82 million in renovations.

The ballpark has no distinct features, but Reinsdorf negotiated his way into getting the first major sports facility built in Chicago since the Chicago Stadium opened in 1929.

In 2003, the naming rights to the new Comiskey Park were sold to U.S. Cellular, which agreed to pay $68 million over a 20-year period. The following year, eight rows and about 6,000 seats were trimmed from the top of the upper deck.

The latest facility battle involves moving the White Sox's spring-training home in Arizona from Tucson to Glendale, a northeast suburb of Phoenix.

The proposed move has rattled some Tucson citizens because they approved funding for a facility that the White Sox have shared with the Arizona Diamondbacks since 1998.

But the White Sox gradually realized that a move to the Valley would dramatically accommodate their fan base, since several thousand White Sox supporters from the Midwest reside in the Phoenix area. The Sox plan to share a facility with the Los Angeles Dodgers.

CONTRACT CONTRADICTIONS

Reinsdorf's stature as a baseball owner in the 1990s was overshadowed by the perception he was working behind the scenes in drawing the hard-line stance against the Major League Baseball

Players Association that led to the 1994 players' strike. At the time, the White Sox were leading the American League Central with a 67–46 record.

"I was torn because of Jerry being so loyal to me, but there were things in baseball that probably weren't fair then," Greg Walker said. "So it worked out and I've never talked to Jerry about it, but his input led to a lot of great things in baseball.

"I'm sure owners at the time and the union had their ideas, but it was a tough time. I don't think the players appreciate what went on back then. It was tough."

In contrast to his hard-line stance, it was Reinsdorf that signed controversial slugger Albert Belle to a stunning five-year, $55 million contract before the 1997 season. The contract was the richest in history at the time and allowed other stars to demand more money from their teams, including Barry Bonds in San Francisco and Sammy Sosa with the Cubs.

More recently, Reinsdorf has shown remarkable generosity in allowing general manager Kenny Williams to expand the player payroll. After the 2005 World Series championship season, the White Sox's payroll increased by $25 million to about $100 million, although about 10 percent of the money came from Philadelphia and Arizona in trades for Jim Thome and Javier Vazquez.

He also stretched an elastic budget further to re-sign slugger Paul Konerko to a five-year, $60 million contract about one month after Konerko gave Reinsdorf the game ball from the final out of the 2005 World Series.

MAN OF THE PEOPLE

Reinsdorf serves on various baseball boards, but he doesn't overlook the best interests and loyalty of his employees and those who have preceded them.

After the White Sox won the 2005 World Series, Reinsdorf gave rings to every full-time employee. For added measure, Mary Frances Veeck, the widow of former owner Bill Veeck, Charles Comiskey, and John Allyn each received a ring.

Those rings were made of 14-karat yellow gold with a 14-karat white gold insert. Each ring was comprised of 95 diamonds of different sizes.

During Reinsdorf's regime, White Sox Charities has donated $2 million to the Chicago Park District and has offered support to the Special Olympics and funding youth fields.

And Reinsdorf has been a big supporter of the Professional Baseball Scouts Foundation, an organization that aids scouts who have lost their jobs, suffer from illness, or encounter other monetary setbacks.

The group was founded by longtime White Sox scout Dave Yoakum, former White Sox GM Roland Hemond, and Dennis Gilbert, a former agent who serves as a special assistant to Reinsdorf.

Under Reinsdorf, the Sox rank among baseball leaders in the Diverse Business Partners Program, in which teams spend several hundred million dollars in goods and services from minority- and female-owned businesses.

"I don't know what his selection process is," Walker said of how one enters into Reinsdorf's White Sox family. "All I know is that he's a lot smarter than I am. I'm happy I was chosen as one of them to be loyal to. I can't tell you how loyal he has been to me. That's rare in professional sports, and I don't think he gets enough credit. I think he gets blamed for it sometimes, which is fairly stupid."

DRAFT DOOZIES

As maddening as the White Sox's inability to win consecutive championships is their failure to convert first-round picks into front-line players (outside of the McDowell-Ventura-Thomas-Fernandez run).

Even as amateur scouting has become more expansive through summer tournaments and fall leagues, the Sox haven't sustained any semblance of long-term success in their selection of No. 1 picks.

PUTTING THE "ILL" IN ILLINOIS

After losing 106 games in 1970, the White Sox had the No. 1 overall pick the following June. The Sox selected Peoria Central High School catcher Danny Goodwin—then failed to sign him. Four years later, Goodwin was drafted by the California Angels—again as the No. 1 overall pick—and played parts of seven nondescript seasons with the Angels, Twins, and A's.

Slugger Jim Rice and pitchers Frank Tanana and Rick Rhoden were selected later in the first round.

The White Sox took Northwestern pitcher Grady Hall in 1986, but Hall advanced only as far as Triple A.

There was plenty of local hype in 2001 when Providence High pitcher Kris Honel was selected as the 16th overall pick. Honel made impressive strides during his first three minor league seasons, striking out 160 in 158⅔ innings at Class A. But arm injuries stunted his progress, and he never regained his velocity and briefly retired during the 2007 season before signing with the St. Louis organization in 2008.

Larry Monroe, an adviser to the baseball department, was the eighth overall selection out of Forest View High in Arlington Heights in 1974 and reached the majors in two years. He pitched in eight games but never returned to the majors.

Of the Sox's five in-state first-round picks, only Steve Trout (Thornwood High) excelled.

WHAT IF?

In 1985, the White Sox selected California high school catcher Kurt Brown with their first pick after B.J. Surhoff, Will Clark, Bobby Witt, and Barry Larkin were selected. After Brown, the next picks were Barry Bonds and Pete Incaviglia. Walt Weiss and Rafael Palmeiro went later in the first round.

Eighteen picks after the White Sox took Brown, a dependable infielder was selected by San Diego—current White Sox bench coach Joey Cora.

As for Brown, he finally reached Triple A in his seventh and final minor league season and finished with a .243 minor league batting average. Brown, however, has devoted his career to helping develop potential prospects as an instructor.

The Sox rolled the dice in 1992 by selecting Eddie Pearson, a 6'3", 285-pound first baseman from little-known Bishop State Community College in Mobile, Alabama. Pearson reached double digits in home runs only twice in eight minor league seasons and finished his playing career in the independent Northern League.

Oregon State pitcher Scott Christman was the 17th overall selection in 1993, but he advanced only as high as Double A before ending his professional career after the 1997 season. Torii Hunter was selected three picks later by American League Central rival Minnesota, where he became a longtime White Sox nemesis before signing a five-year, $90 million contract with the Los Angeles Angels despite general manager Kenny Williams' long-time affection and attempts to sign him.

Six years later, the White Sox went to the Northwest again to take pitcher Jason Stumm out of Centralia, Washington. Stumm was one of the highest-rated pitchers coming out of the draft, but he needed reconstructive elbow surgery less than two years later. A bone spur in his pitching elbow and a torn rotator cuff stunted his development and he ended his career after the 2005 season without reaching Triple A.

The Sox didn't have a top-10 pick from 1991 (when Baylor pitcher Scott Ruffcorn was the 25th overall selection) until 2008, when they drafted Georgia shortstop Gordon Beckham with the eighth overall pick and gave him a $2.6 million bonus.

THE BORAS FACTOR

The White Sox could have drafted Jason Varitek, who was taken four picks after they selected Scott Christman in 1993. But that probably would have accelerated the acrimony that swelled between the club and agent Scott Boras, who served as Varitek's family adviser at the time. Varitek didn't sign with Minnesota despite being the Twins' second first-round pick (after Torii Hunter) and returned to Georgia Tech. He moved up seven spots in the 1994 draft when he was drafted by Seattle.

But in 1996, Boras found a loophole when he discovered the White Sox hadn't made an official contract offer to first-round pick Bobby Seay within 15 days after Seay was selected as the 12th overall pick. Seay was ruled a free agent and signed with Tampa Bay, not far from his Sarasota, Florida, residence.

One year later, the White Sox failed to reach an agreement with Fresno State pitcher Jeff Weaver, a second-round pick who was advised by Boras. Weaver returned to FSU and was the 14th overall selection of Detroit and reached the majors in 1999.

That was the same year the White Sox failed to sign second-round pick Bobby Hill out of the University of Miami. Boras steered Hill toward Newark of the independent Atlantic League, and the Cubs selected Hill in the second round of the 2002 draft, 23 spots ahead of where the White Sox picked him in 1999.

The White Sox drafted Texas junior outfielder Jordan Danks in the seventh round of the 2008 draft, but that came shortly after Danks dumped Boras as his family adviser in favor of Jeff Berry.

The Sox signed Danks to a $525,000 bonus, well above the standard bonus for that slot. That's been a rarity for the Sox since they gave Stanford outfielder/quarterback Joe Borchard a $5.3 million bonus as their first-round pick in 2000. Borchard failed to live up to the money or the expectations of a first-round pick, and the Sox have been perceived in the industry as taking "safe" picks with college players since Borchard and pitcher Kris Honel were taken in consecutive years.

Before general manager Kenny Williams fired scouting director Duane Shaffer two weeks after the 2007 draft, one of the few things they had in common was their preference not to select players advised by Boras.

While much of the scrutiny around the White Sox and Boras in recent years has revolved around All-Star third baseman Joe Crede and his free agency after the 2008 season, Boras has tried to defuse the level of hatred.

"My philosophy is that I've had players who have signed multiyear contracts and players who have signed one-year deals," Boras said in May 2007. "And we're all ears as we listen to things. If Joe thinks there's something we ought to do, we do it. There was a situation last year where we had a very amicable negotiation last winter with the Sox on a one-year basis.

"There are a lot of things written in Chicago that have no foundation from my point of view and my relationship with that franchise. Whenever I've called Jerry Reinsdorf, he's called me back. Whenever I've called Kenny, he's called me back. Obviously, sometimes you have different opinions about value if I have a player with the White Sox."

DRAFT DOMINANCE

The late 1980s were rough at the major league level for the White Sox, but they struck gold with their first-round draft picks in four consecutive years with marquee players.

It also was a testament to the scouting department, as it was their homework that led to each selection.

Jack McDowell

After the second pick in the 1987 draft, eight consecutive pitchers were selected. The White Sox, with the fifth overall selection, needed a fast-track pitcher to help the major league roster as soon as possible.

Jack McDowell was as polished as any pitcher in the draft, with the arguable exception of Cal State Fullerton's Mike Harkey, who was taken fourth by the Cubs.

Jack McDowell went 22–10 in 1993 and won the AL Cy Young Award.

McDowell hailed from the same hometown as former Los Angeles Dodgers great Don Drysdale, and like Big D, McDowell wasn't afraid to throw inside, even at the college level. McDowell also featured a split-finger fastball to go with his mid-90s fastball.

He even held the distinction of snapping Robin Ventura's 58-game hitting streak in a College World Series game and gained revenge for losing to Ventura's Oklahoma State Cowboys by beating them on two days' rest in the championship game.

McDowell became an instant success as a freshman in 1985 with future major leaguers Jeff Ballard and Pete Stanicek, and he credited much of his accelerated success to legendary Stanford coach Mark Marquess.

"The great thing about playing for Coach Marquess at Stanford was they teach the whole game, and I don't think that gets covered a lot with pitchers," McDowell said. "Pitchers kind of do their own thing and they don't learn the little aspects about playing the game of baseball, which we did at Stanford. That helps in the long run. You know what guys are trying to do around you. You know what works, what doesn't. You know what the running game is all about. But it gives you that extra step to be ready to play."

McDowell was among the first of several front-line starting pitchers under Cardinal pitching coach Tom Dunton, who later served briefly as a minor league coach with Oakland before retiring. Dunton also helped develop Mike Mussina, Rick Helling, and Kyle Peterson—all first-round picks.

"He had a great overall knowledge of the game, not just the pitching end of it, but what everyone else is trying to do around you," McDowell said. "And that prepares you as much as anything to take that step up to play the game at the level the big leagues are at."

About three months after pitching Stanford to its first NCAA baseball title, McDowell made his major league debut for the White Sox and went on to pitch 12 major league seasons.

Robin Ventura

Robin Ventura was no secret heading into the 1988 draft, based on his hitting streak the previous year for one of the nation's top programs. U.S. Olympic coach Mark Marquess showed no favoritism when he selected Ventura as the starting third baseman over Ed Sprague, who helped Stanford to two national championships and had more power potential than Ventura.

Four of Ventura's U.S. Olympic teammates were taken ahead of him in the 1988 draft. With the ninth overall pick, the Cubs took second base speedster Ty Griffin of Georgia Tech. That paved the way for the White Sox to select Ventura, who slid to the 10th overall pick despite hitting .428 with 302 RBIs during his three seasons at OSU.

Ventura was selected ahead of five more Olympic players in the first round, as well as a highly touted pitcher from Monsignor Pace High School in Miami named Alex Fernandez.

Robin Ventura was a fixture at third base for the White Sox during his 10 years in Chicago.

Because the Olympics didn't end until the fall, Ventura couldn't start his professional career until 1989. But he received a September promotion and remained in the majors until the end of the 2004 season. He won six Gold Glove Awards for his defense with the White Sox.

Frank Thomas

Chicago-area native Mike Rizzo was assigned to scout prospects in Alabama, Mississippi, Georgia, and Florida and became transfixed on a former Auburn tight end named Frank Thomas.

Thomas didn't make the 1988 U.S. Olympic team, but the White Sox's talent evaluators loved Thomas' impact potential.

"Al Goldis and Larry Himes were focused on Frank throughout the process," recalled Rizzo, who later drafted the nucleus for the 2007 NL Western Division champion Arizona Diamondbacks before taking a job as the chief evaluator for the Washington Nationals.

The White Sox loved Thomas despite reports from the Major League Scouting Bureau that weren't as glowing as their own.

"We were taking a chance," Rizzo recalled. "All we heard was 'All he can do is hit.' But he could throw, run, play defense, and have a chance to hit .300 with 30 home runs, draw his walks, and take his pitches. We also liked his makeup as a football guy."

The White Sox were concerned that Thomas could be difficult to sign because of his leverage as a college junior, but Rizzo was convinced that Thomas could become a major player.

There also was another consideration. Outfielder Jeff Jackson, from Simeon High School on Chicago's South Side, was a projected top-five pick. The White Sox worked Jackson out in the event he slipped to the seventh overall pick and would have faced local pressure to select him if he was available.

"I liked Jeff Jackson," said Phil Rizzo, the Sox's Chicago-area scout and Mike Rizzo's father. "Jackson had a hell of a body. Frank was a college guy. Fantastic power, who knows what he was going to do, but he was big enough that you knew he was going to do something. Defensively, where was he going to play? That was the thing.

In his first full season with the Sox, Frank Thomas hit .318, slugged 32 home runs, and knocked in 109 runs.

"Jeff Jackson could do it all—play center field, run like a deer, and had a great body. Beautiful body.... We worked the kid [Jackson] out and made him take his shirt off. He was what you call 'body beautiful.' If he was a girl, he could have been a movie star. That's the funny thing about this game, you never know. But at the time with the White Sox, you want to move fast, you want to win right away, you take the college kid."

With three years of Southeastern Conference baseball under his belt, Thomas became a more clear choice for the Sox, and any local pressure was alleviated when Philadelphia took Jackson three spots ahead of Thomas and signed him.

"Frank was the culmination of a lot of hard work," Mike Rizzo said. "You have to remember that he wasn't a big consensus guy. But we knew that because of his production and because he was a college player, he was ahead of a lot of kids. We saw him as an impact bat. He was more of a hitter-with-power hitter. We looked at him closely that fall [at Auburn in 1988] and saw that he was athletic enough to take."

Thomas appreciated the schooling he received at the high school and college levels to make him an all-around hitter.

"I always hit," Thomas said. "I had some good coaches before I got to the majors. My high school coach, Bobby Howard, was a great coach. Then I got with Steve Renfroe [at Auburn], who was a pretty good hitting guy. He was one coach who really broke out on fundamentals."

Thomas reached the majors shortly after the one-year anniversary of his selection by the Sox.

Jackson, meanwhile, reached only as far as Double A with Philadelphia.

Alex Fernandez

Alex Fernandez was such an impressive player at an early age that he played third base for Monsignor Pace High School in Miami as an eighth grader.

ESPN reporter Pedro Gomez covered Fernandez for the now-defunct *Miami News* and said that eighth graders in Florida could play high school baseball if they attended private schools such as Pace.

Fernandez attended a private school despite living in the Hialeah High attendance district, which produced the likes of former White Sox shortstop Bucky Dent, Pro Football Hall of Fame linebacker Ted Hendricks, and Harry Casey of KC and the Sunshine Band.

"The only caveat to the rule was that eighth graders were not allowed to pitch for the high school team," Gomez recalled. "But Alex was a phenom, and they usually batted him third on that state title team.

"I know that Alex was a stud third baseman at Pace when he wasn't on the mound. The guy was their cleanup hitter from his freshman through senior year. He routinely batted over .500 and probably could have made it as a third baseman. He had power

Pitcher Alex Fernandez
posted a 79–63 record
as a member of the White Sox.

and could hit for average. But pitching being at such a premium, that's what the clubs wanted."

Milwaukee selected Fernandez with the 24th overall selection in the 1988 draft, and Gomez was at the Fernandez house where champagne bottles popped after he received a call from the Brewers.

But the celebration stopped when the Brewers didn't meet Fernandez's demands.

"It was typical Brewers back then—lowball and see if the kid would sign," Gomez said. "Alex had options and didn't care."

Fernandez elected to attend the University of Miami and compiled a 15–2 record and 2.01 ERA as a freshman. But since four-year college players weren't eligible for the draft until after their junior year, Fernandez elected to transfer to Miami-Dade Community College for his sophomore season.

At 6'1" and 215 pounds, Fernandez was close to being a finished product. The Sox, still looking for fast-track players, took Fernandez with the fourth overall selection in 1990.

Although Mike Mussina was selected 16 spots after Fernandez and was still pitching in 2008, Fernandez proved to be one of the Sox's best selections. Fernandez needed only six professional starts before he was promoted to the majors by the end of the 1990 season.

The Sox would go 18 seasons before they would have another top-10 selection. And when they took Georgia shortstop Gordon Beckham with the eighth overall pick in the 2008 draft, Fernandez represented the White Sox at Major League Baseball's draft headquarters in Orlando, Florida.

INTERNATIONALLY SPEAKING

The 2005 White Sox had a tremendous international flavor on baseball's biggest stage. But the roots started to grow half a century before their crowning achievement.

CUBAN CONNECTION
Minnie Minoso

Orestes "Minnie" Minoso still visits U.S. Cellular Field with a smile and a bounce in his step, nearly 60 years after joining the White Sox following a trade from Cleveland.

Minoso is one of the reasons why foreign players have always fit in so well with the White Sox. When he wasn't working in the sugar fields, Minoso played his way through the minor leagues in Cuba and initially passed up a chance to play in the United States, opting instead for the Mexican League.

Minoso helped cultivate the "Go-Go White Sox" image by stealing 31 bases in 1951. He instantly added pizzazz to the franchise with his array of talents and finished fourth in the American League MVP balloting in both 1953 and 1954.

Minoso always found a way to help his team, as evidenced by him leading the league in getting hit by pitches for six consecutive seasons, including a franchise-record 23 times in 1956. Minoso had an impressive .425 on-base percentage that year.

Minnie Minoso's No. 9 was retired by the Sox in 1983.

Minoso was traded the season before the White Sox reached the World Series but returned in 1960, batting .311 and .280 in successive seasons.

But as his speed declined, so did his production. After a two-year stint in St. Louis and Washington, Minoso joined the White Sox for a third time in 1964 but was released at midseason and missed their unsuccessful pennant-stretch drive.

Part of Minoso's legacy was tarnished in 1976 when owner Bill Veeck activated him in September after serving most of the season as a coach, thus enabling Minoso to achieve the distinction of playing in four decades. Minoso was activated again in 1980 and went hitless in two at-bats. A similar ploy in 1993 was abandoned.

Although Minoso has a statue at U.S. Cellular Field, he was accidentally denied admittance to the White Sox's clubhouse during their World Series celebration at Minute Maid Park in Houston.

"They won't let me in; they say they don't know who I am," Minoso said while reporters, players' wives, kids, and members of the White Sox's organization were admitted.

Jose Contreras

Jose Contreras marked one of the greatest reclamation projects in White Sox history. His success also speaks to the support system that continues to aid foreign players.

After defecting from the Cuban National Team during a tournament in Mexico in September 2002, the "Bronze Titan" failed to live up to the hype after signing with the New York Yankees.

Contreras had a 117–50 career record that prompted the Yankees, despite a fierce recruitment by the rival Red Sox, to sign him to a four-year, $32 million contract.

But the Yankees failed to receive instant results from the hard-throwing, 6'4", 245-pound right-hander. The main gripe was that Contreras relied more on his split-finger fastball than his 95-mph fastball, even on 3–2 counts.

General manager Kenny Williams, who has frequently kept an eye on the future despite his sense of urgency to win now, bought low when he dealt former AL All-Star Esteban Loaiza to the Yankees in a July 31, 2004, deadline deal for Contreras, whom the Yankees deemed wasn't going to help them in their drive to reach the playoffs.

Part of Williams' thinking was that a bilingual manager (Ozzie Guillen) and a pitching coach who also spoke Spanish and was effective at maximizing talents (Don Cooper) could help Contreras reach his potential.

To contribute to Contreras' support system, Williams signed fellow Cuban Orlando "El Duque" Hernandez to a two-year contract to fortify the pitching staff as well as make Contreras feel more comfortable.

The Sox never lost faith in Contreras despite his 4–5 record and 4.26 ERA at the All-Star break in 2005. The biggest boost, however, came from Hernandez, who suggested that Contreras drop his arm angle to make him more formidable against right-handed hitters.

The move resulted in an 11–2 record that carried the Sox to the World Series and elevated him to staff-ace status. The ability to pitch on a big stage also enabled Contreras to dismiss accusations he couldn't perform under pressure.

Contreras carried that success into the first half of 2006, when he extended a regular-season winning streak to a franchise-record 17 games (it was eventually stopped at Yankee Stadium).

A divorce and arm fatigue ate away at Contreras in 2007 and cast some doubts as to whether he was washed up.

He responded with a fresh mind while also polishing his English-speaking skills after noticing that his teenage daughters, Naylan and Naylenis, learned the language quickly.

Jose Contreras won 17 straight decisions for the White Sox during the 2005 and 2006 seasons.

Unfortunately for Contreras, an Achilles tendon injury on August 11 ended his 2008 season. But his success and happiness in Chicago helped the Sox land another Cuban import.

Alexei Ramirez

There were plenty of questions before Alexei Ramirez arrived in Tucson for spring training in 2008. But Contreras and agent Jaime Torres helped answer them.

Contreras and Ramirez played briefly in Cuba for Pinar Del Rio, but Contreras vividly remembered witnessing Ramirez's all-around skills before defecting.

The White Sox based their opinions of Ramirez on scouting reports from international tournaments, videotapes, and Contreras' input. In fact, Williams has often sought Contreras' opinion on several Cuban players, and Contreras could easily work as a scout based on some of the evaluations he has made—particularly those that steered the White Sox away from signing some defectors who have subsequently failed to live up to their billing elsewhere.

During a lunch session at the winter meetings held in the spacious Opryland Hotel in Nashville, Torres did his best to convince Williams that Ramirez would be a great fit in Chicago. Former top talent evaluator David Wilder, along with scouts from several teams, watched Ramirez during a workout in the Dominican Republic.

Ramirez didn't consider himself a defector because his wife was a Dominican Republic citizen studying medicine in Cuba. But Ramirez considered himself ready for the majors and embarked on his pursuit.

The Sox didn't have a true position for Ramirez, but signed him to a four-year, $4.75 million contract.

It could turn out to be one of the best signings in Sox history.

Manager Ozzie Guillen believed Ramirez was too talented to not be on the major league roster despite his lack of big-league experience. That proved true when Ramirez, whose best positions are shortstop and center field, took over at second base for an injured Juan Uribe.

In his first start after Uribe got hurt, Ramirez hit his first major league home run May 16 off San Francisco's Jonathan Sanchez and ran away with the starting position.

Ramirez's blend of power, speed, and defensive agility prompted Guillen to name Ramirez "the Cuban Missile." He finished second in the voting for the 2008 AL Rookie of the Year Award.

In December 2008, the Sox signed another Cuban star, 19-year-old Dayan Viciedo, to a four-year, $10 million deal. The team hopes Viciedo will claim the starting spot at third base or make a smooth transition to playing left field.

VENEZUELAN PRIDE
Chico the Man

Manager Ozzie Guillen was disheartened when he couldn't fly home to attend the funeral of Chico Carrasquel in May 2005.

Carrasquel, like Guillen, did not start his career with the White Sox. General manager Frank Lane acquired Carrasquel from the Brooklyn Dodgers' organization, and Carrasquel did his best talking on the field after replacing Hall of Fame shortstop Luke Appling in 1950.

Carrasquel batted .282 in his rookie season in 1950 that included a 24-game hitting streak. He played only six seasons before moving on to Cleveland, but his ability to make a successful transition made the White Sox a popular team in his homeland. In 1951, Carrasquel became the first Latin player to start in the All-Star Game.

During Guillen's first homestand as manager of the White Sox in April 2004, the team arranged for Carrasquel, Luis Aparicio, and Guillen to throw the ceremonial first pitches. Guillen was involved in the selection as a tribute to those he felt helped him land his position.

He also tried to aid Carrasquel, who was attempting to get out of his wheelchair.

"He said, 'Don't hold me. I will get up.' It was amazing. He had just come from physical therapy, and I know he was in bad shape on that particular day. But just to have him there was great," Guillen said.

Carrasquel passed away in May 2005, several months before the White Sox's World Series triumph. Before Game 1 of the 2005 American League Championship Series, Guillen was asked at a news conference what Carrasquel would have thought about the White Sox's accomplishments.

"You're going to make me cry," Guillen said as he rolled his knuckles and left the podium before breaking down.

Guillen was more at ease 10 days later about his feelings toward Carrasquel.

"The thing I feel bad about is that he never had the opportunity to see this," Guillen said. "He never had the chance to enjoy this. I know where he is right now at this particular moment. In the meanwhile, he wishes us to be the best we can be.

"That's why I was kind of sensitive about it. I always think about how bad he wanted this for the city of Chicago, for himself, for a lot of people. He was truly a baseball fan. When I was asked about it, the first thing that came to my mind was that he was so disappointed that it might be the last year he might get to see it. All of a sudden, a lot of people were going to enjoy this instead of him."

Luis Aparacio

Coincidentally, it was Aparacio who replaced his Venezuelan hero Carrasquel at shortstop. Unlike his father, Luis Sr., the younger Aparicio elected to leave his homeland to pursue a major league career.

After two stints with the White Sox that covered 10 years, 1,513 games, and 318 stolen bases, Aparicio was honored at Comiskey Park in 1984—the same year he was inducted into the Hall of Fame.

Ozzie Guillen

Guillen was scouted by well-respected San Diego Padres scouts including Sandy Johnson, Dick Hager, and Luis Rosa long before Jerry Krause worked endless hours to acquire him for the Sox.

Three generations of Venezuelan White Sox shortstops: Luis Aparicio, Ozzie Guillen, and Chico Carrasquel.

"I was lucky," Guillen said. "I always believed in destiny, and that was my destiny. It's funny because I grew up watching Carrasquel manage Venezuelan players. When you talk about Aparicio and Carrasquel, those are our Hall of Famers. And Chico was our dad. And when you talk about Chico, everyone liked Chico. And everyone respected Luis. There were two different things—love and respect.

"And I grew up in Little League with Luis Aparicio's uncle, Ernesto. And wow, how did everything come up."

Guillen said he signed with San Diego because of Ernesto, who was working for the Padres.

"And all of a sudden, all the destiny. Wow. I played with the team where Luis had his best years. And I remember telling my wife [Ibis] in Triple A [in 1984], 'I was supposed to be traded to the Dodgers and Philadelphia.' And I remember Ozzie Jr. was just born. And we're decorating Ozzie's room with baseball things. And I remember there was the Winning Ugly team, and I told my wife, 'I wish I could play for them,'" Guillen said.

ASIAN PERSUASION
Shingo Takatsu

Although Shingo Takatsu lasted less than two seasons with the Sox, he was one of the first to demonstrate Japan's influence on the White Sox.

In 2004, Kenny Williams sought to fortify a bullpen that featured struggling closer Billy Koch, who had been acquired from Oakland in a trade for Keith Foulke in 2002. Williams became very curious after watching Takatsu's deceptive sidearm delivery that produced 260 saves in 13 seasons and earned him the nickname "Mr. Zero" in Japan.

Takatsu took advantage of Koch's struggles to immediately become the White Sox's closer during the 2004 season. Takatsu finished second in the American League Rookie of the Year voting with 19 saves and a 2.31 ERA in 59 appearances. He became a fan favorite and was greeted by the loud sound of a gong when he entered games at U.S. Cellular Field.

The only warning sign in 2004 occurred in August, when Takatsu had a 7.36 ERA in 11 appearances. He rebounded in September, but his struggles in 2005 resurfaced and he was released with two months left in the season.

Tadahito Iguchi

A year after signing Takatsu, Williams opened the White Sox's wallet to sign Iguchi, who batted a modest .271 with 149 home runs and 159 stolen bases in eight seasons with the Fukuoka Daiei Hawks of the Japanese Pacific League.

Iguchi remained reserved but let his performance speak for himself. He proved to be a great fit in the second spot with his unselfishness and bat control that enabled leadoff hitter Scott Podsednik to steal 59 bases and kick-start a White Sox offense that had relied heavily on the home run in previous seasons.

Iguchi seemed calm with Japanese reporters and warmed up to beat writers, and he felt comfortable living in Arlington Heights with its large Japanese community.

Several times manager Ozzie Guillen referred to Iguchi as the most valuable player during the White Sox's stretch drive because of his ability to work with double-play partner Juan Uribe, who spoke little English.

Iguchi came through with one of the biggest hits of the 2005 postseason, smacking a grand slam off Boston left-hander David Wells to win Game 2 of the AL Division Series.

Iguchi played one and a half more seasons with the Sox before he was dealt to Philadelphia, where Chase Utley had suffered a broken wrist. Iguchi helped the Phillies reach the playoffs while instantly winning over tough-minded fans.

IN SICKNESS AND IN HEALTH

BO KNOWS HERM

Herm Schneider had seen it all, even before he joined the White Sox as head trainer in 1979. Before moving to Chicago, Schneider served as an assistant trainer for the New York Yankees during the Bronx Zoo years capped by consecutive world championships in 1977 and 1978.

But in 1991, Sox general manager Ron Schueler presented the venerable Schneider with one of his greatest challenges—rehabbing injured NFL Pro Bowl running back Bo Jackson.

The White Sox were able to take a chance on Jackson, a 1989 American League All-Star, only because Jackson had a football career–ending hip injury known as avascular necrosis that caused the Kansas City Royals to release him.

"I remember we were in spring training in Sarasota [in 1991], and Schu called me aside and said we had acquired Bo and he wanted me to fix him," Schneider recalled.

"I looked at him like, 'Fix him?' I don't know I've ever fixed a person with a hip that's been damaged that badly. And that's a tough thing to fix. In short, normally you take a square peg and try to fit it in a square hole or a round peg in a round hole. We were trying to fit a round peg in a square hole. It's very difficult to do. But we tried."

Schneider and Jackson quickly bonded and worked endlessly as the White Sox began their 1991 season. By the start of

September, Jackson was healthy enough to play but faced the bigger task of trying to get ready for an entire season.

Jackson spent the entire winter rehabbing the hip and then going to the Illinois Institute of Technology to perform baseball functional drills.

At the time, the White Sox believed that Jackson could be ready to play first base but that his hip would prevent him from playing the outfield. But when spring training arrived in 1992, the pain was too obvious even for that, and Schneider recommended Jackson undergo further tests on the hip.

"Finally, he and I had a talk," said Schneider. He recalled telling Jackson, "'Bo, for the quality of your life, take baseball out of it.' Because everything he was doing, from putting on his shoes to putting on his socks, trying to put on his trousers, sleeping at night—everything was giving him trouble. So he couldn't put on his socks, couldn't put on his shoes, couldn't put on his pants. I said, 'Bo, for the quality of your life, we need to rethink this and talk about getting a total hip put in. Let's not do it for the wrong reasons. Let's do it for the right reasons. The right reasons are so you can live a normal life. You're a young guy. It's a little early in your life to get a hip, but the amount of pain you're in and the stuff you like to do...'"

Jackson agreed, but he left a telling message to his friends before having surgery.

"He called everyone aside and said, 'Thanks for your support and everything else, but I got to get this hip done. But I will see you again,'" Schneider recalled.

The surgery was performed on April 4—Schneider's birthday—and Jackson gradually felt better, even though the intent of the operation was not to get him back on the baseball field.

But Jackson felt so much better after the pain subsided that he approached Schneider about playing again. After several discussions that involved Schneider, Jackson's wife, Linda, Dr. James Andrews, and other specialists, Jackson was cleared to embark on his next comeback.

"These were uncharted waters," Schneider said. "Because what you have to know about an artificial hip, more than what to do,

Bo Jackson hit 19 home runs in 108 games for the White Sox in 1991 and 1993.

is what *not* to do. There are certain things that can take the hip and throw it out.

"I got involved in that and learned about things that would put him in harm's way and we would certainly stay away from that, best we could. And we proceeded and kept working and working until the wintertime. And once winter came, we went back to working on baseball stuff again and he still was at first base because it was easier."

Jackson's movement progressed to the point that he began simulated baseball drills at IIT.

To break up the monotony of a serious rehab during the depressing winter months, Schneider would pick his spots to keep Jackson loose.

"We'd return from IIT to U.S. Cellular Field, and I'd drive his truck," Schneider recalled. "I'd turn the wheel, hit the brakes, and do doughnuts. He was great about it."

Jackson kept his focus and passed all the tests leading up to spring training, with a sliding hurdle awaiting him.

"That was a big challenge," said Schneider, who had Jackson practice sliding but needed him to slide in an exhibition game spontaneously and correctly.

That test came in Bradenton, Florida, against Pittsburgh, and Jackson performed a pop-up slide at second.

"He looked at me and said, 'Look at that!'" Schneider recalled.

In Jackson's first game on April 9, 1993, he hit a pinch-hit home run against the New York Yankees. He finished the season with 16 home runs and was part of the White Sox's American League West championship team.

Although the Sox released Jackson after the '93 season, he and Schneider have remained close.

"I know a lot of people who would feel sorry for themselves, who would try to put the blame on others for this happening, or say, 'Why does this have to happen for me? In the prime of my career, why did this have to happen to me?'" Schneider said. "I never ever heard [Bo] say anything like that. Never."

FIXING A FLAT ON THE VENTURA HIGHWAY

"Very gruesome," was the way Schneider described Robin Ventura's season-threatening right ankle break and dislocation in an exhibition game on March 21, 1997.

Ventura slid across home plate and caught his foot in the mud, causing an injury that nearly put him in total shock as Schneider implored him to relax.

"If it was another strange person or somebody he didn't know, he would have been scared to death, and he was already scared," Schneider said.

"For a long time, I thought I wasn't going to come back [in 1997]," Ventura recalled. "Herm kept pushing me."

Ventura, 29, was at the prime of his outstanding career but faced the prospect of missing an entire season. That caused Schneider and his staff to find creative ways to accelerate the healing process. One included cutting windows on his cast where muscle stimulators could be applied to regenerate the bone.

"I was really thinking outside the box," Schneider recalled. "We were trying things to get rid of the swelling, reeducate the muscles, and trying to keep it together. He was terrific to work with.

"That's the only way these things really work, if you get the person who is willing to have the will to come back, the will to work, the will to listen, and the will to put up with a lot of [stuff] from me. There was a lot of work, a lot of pain, a lot of misery."

Schneider engrained in Ventura's mind that the rehab was extremely tough so that if he had an easy day, "It's frosting on the cake."

Had Ventura stuck with a traditional rehab based on the RICE theory—rest, ice, compression, and elevation—Schneider thought the recovery might not have gone as smoothly. Because the leg was in a cast, Ventura had to cope with muscle atrophy and stiffness.

The aggressive approach enabled Ventura to work on his rehabilitation sooner because much of the muscle had started to return and the swelling had subsided.

Like Bo Jackson, one of Ventura's biggest tests involved sliding—the same act that led to his injury.

"But I told him, 'You just can't think about it,'" Schneider said. "'I know that's easy for me to say and not easy for you to do, but we have to really talk about it, get through it.' Finally, he was okay with it. But we started talking about it. It's almost like when you get thrown off a horse, they tell you to get back on.

"We started talking about this as an accident. He slid a million times, and nothing's ever happened. One time it happens. You look at it as an accident. It was a matter of trying to get that fear out of his head."

Schneider had a special brace made for Ventura's ankle but made sure that he took the brace off Ventura so he could ensure the ankle was healing properly.

Just four months after fracturing and dislocating the ankle, Ventura returned on July 24 and hit a game-winning double in his first game back with the Sox.

Ventura played one more season with the White Sox before signing with the New York Mets as a free agent, and Schneider's work helped him play through the 2004 season. Ventura played

161 games with the Sox in 1998 and the same amount the following season with the Mets, who trusted Schneider's medical work enough to give Ventura a four-year, $32 million contract.

Ventura also won Gold Glove Awards for his superb defense in the two years following his surgery.

TOUGH LOVE FOR OZZIE

Shortstop Ozzie Guillen had played in at least 149 games in each of his first seven major league seasons, and there seemed to be little that could slow him down.

But a collision with left fielder Tim Raines on April 21, 1992, resulted in torn ligaments in Guillen's knee that sidelined him for the season and created another task for Schneider.

"I kept him here in the winter and wouldn't let him go to Venezuela," Schneider recalled.

Those weren't the worst words Guillen heard while on the operating table.

"I told Ozzie, 'Tell me now if you don't want to work at this, because if you don't want to work at this, you're done,'" Schneider said. "'If you want to work at this, I'll get you right.'"

Schneider added that Guillen faced a "terrible" rehab and that he was going to challenge him while others would be afraid to do the same because they didn't want to jeopardize their friendship.

For more motivation, Guillen would rehab his knee at the same time Bo Jackson was preparing for his comeback after hip surgery.

"I'd challenge Ozzie by saying, 'Look what Bo's doing. You're telling me you can't do it when he's doing it?'" Schneider said.

Guillen's rehabilitation wasn't on the "superhighway," as Schneider describes it. Tearing the scar tissue to straighten out his leg was similar to "sticking a knife in his heart," Schneider said. "It was that bad."

But the work paid off. Guillen returned in 1993 with a .280 batting average in 134 games, and his career extended into the 2000 season.

JORDAN'S JOURNEY

In the city renown for gambling, Herm Schneider was involved in one of the biggest eye-opening risks taken by a professional athlete at the zenith of his career.

During the baseball meetings in Las Vegas after the 1993 season, chairman Jerry Reinsdorf told Schneider, "I got a special project for you."

"You're not going to believe this, but I want you to get Michael Jordan ready to play baseball," Reinsdorf said.

"I looked at him funny," Schneider recalled. "Are you serious?"

Reinsdorf confirmed that the greatest basketball player in history intended to switch to baseball after announcing his first retirement from the NBA at the age of 30. Reinsdorf told Jordan he would give him a chance, and that Schneider was the perfect person to prepare him.

"He was a driven guy to do this," Schneider said. "I don't understand where he was in his career. I'm not sure if he really quit basketball and wanted to try baseball, or basketball had quit on him for a while."

After winning three consecutive NBA titles, Jordan was ready for a change.

But this had to be kept a secret for as long as possible. Schneider talked to Jordan three times before they embarked on a program that started the Friday after Thanksgiving.

Schneider's three-part plan involved getting Jordan conditioned to play baseball, preparing him for skill work, and then getting him ready to actually play baseball—a sport he hadn't played since high school.

Jordan worked out six days a week. To keep the workouts as quiet as possible, Schneider devised a plan: Jordan would call him when he was five minutes away from U.S. Cellular Field, and Schneider would unlock the chain that would enable Jordan to pull into the park past the television docks before closing the door.

Jordan's hands were calloused from weightlifting, but Schneider knew that his project had to strengthen his shoulders

Michael Jordan worked closely with head trainer Herm Schneider during his aborted attempt to reach the major leagues.

for baseball duties. He also assigned Jordan hand and wrist exercises and rotation work that simulated swinging a bat.

"We had to work both ways so he wouldn't rip a rib muscle," Schneider recalled. "We did a lot of preventive work with him because there was nothing wrong. We just tried to get him tuned up."

When Jordan advanced to the third stage, much of the work shifted to the Illinois Institute of Technology, where he would field ground balls and throw in complete privacy.

Many of the workouts lasted from 9:00 AM to 5:00 PM, with the only delays caused by Jordan's hand bleeding from all the swinging practice.

"These were long days, but this was something he wanted to do," Schneider said. "It was far from a cakewalk."

About three weeks before spring training, Schneider accompanied Jordan on his private plane from Waukegan to Sarasota, Florida, to hit outside.

"We flew over the fields and I told him, 'Those are your new homes now,'" Schneider said with a smile.

Jordan, however, batted only .202 with three home runs, 51 RBIs, and 30 stolen bases as an outfielder for Double-A Birmingham. He memorably doubled in the exhibition Crosstown Classic against the Chicago Cubs and played in the Arizona Fall League before returning to the NBA, where he captured three more league titles and two MVP Awards with the Bulls.

"I'm no baseball expert and don't claim to be, but he survived," Schneider said. "A lot of people who would have tried it probably wouldn't have survived, but he survived."

GENERALLY MANAGING

ew organizations have had a more diverse group of general managers than the last five GMs of the White Sox. Here's a closer look at the men, their backgrounds, and their highs and lows.

ROLAND HEMOND (1971–85)

It would be unfair to call Roland Hemond merely a "baseball lifer." His contributions go well beyond the renaissance he oversaw in 1972 with Dick Allen and Chuck Tanner, the South Side Hitmen in 1977, and the 1983 Winning Ugly team.

Hemond currently serves as a special assistant to Arizona's dynamic president Derrick Hall, who has wisely utilized Hemond's skills in several areas to bring more credibility to the Diamondbacks.

Hemond married into a baseball family. His wife, Margo, is the sister of former GM Bob Quinn, who preached an SDSD approach to building a farm system—scout, draft, sign, and develop.

To some extent, this philosophy applied to Hemond throughout his tenure with the White Sox. But he was largely a man of action, not reaction, from the time he arrived in Chicago after working as the farm director with the California Angels.

According to Arizona's media guide, Hemond made 135 trades involving 428 players while he was with the White Sox and the Baltimore Orioles.

With the Sox, Hemond had no choice but to shake up the roster after inheriting a team that lost 106 games. Familiar with the Angels' talent, Hemond sent center fielder Ken Berry to California in a six-player trade that brought Jay Johnstone, Tom Egan, and Tom Bradley to the Sox.

He also traded Hall of Fame shortstop Luis Aparicio to Boston for Mike Andrews and Luis Alvarado. And before spring training in 1971, Hemond acquired outfielder and former No. 1 pick Rick Reichardt from Washington for pitcher Jerry Janeski.

The 1971 White Sox improved by 23 games, thanks to many of Hemond's moves. But his biggest transaction came nearly two months later when he traded Tommy John and infielder Steve Huntz for Dick Allen, who was playing for his fourth team in four seasons.

Allen promptly hit 37 homers and drove in 113 runs as the White Sox won 87 games in 1972, but finished 5½ games behind eventual World Series champion Oakland in the AL West. The White Sox were in first place as late as August 28 before losing four straight games; the closest they got after that was two games out on September 12.

Unfortunately for Hemond, injuries squandered a 26–14 start in 1973, and Andrews and Reichardt were released later that year.

GM Roland Hemond (right) was the driving force behind many of the most memorable deals in Sox history, including the acquisition of former Cub Ron Santo in 1973.

The peculiar acquisition of Cubs favorite Ron Santo gave the White Sox two strong third basemen but no pitching depth. Their large investment in Allen also hampered efforts to upgrade the pitching staff and resulted in a .500 season (80–80) in 1974.

Hemond was well liked in baseball circles, and perhaps his greatest achievement was being able to work for three owners—John Allyn, Bill Veeck, and Jerry Reinsdorf.

Hemond coped well while Veeck stole the spotlight by pushing Tanner out and hiring 67-year-old Paul Richards; changing the uniforms so players would sport collars and shorts; and bringing Minnie Minoso out of retirement at age 54.

Those stunts couldn't mask a 97-loss season in 1976, and it was Hemond's vision that helped the Sox regain respect—albeit on a short-term basis.

Hemond traded shortstop Bucky Dent to the New York Yankees for outfielder Oscar Gamble and pitcher LaMarr Hoyt before the start of the 1977 season. Earlier, the Sox had acquired power-hitting outfielder Richie Zisk at the cost of Rich Gossage and Terry Forster. Two years earlier, Hemond landed youngster Chet Lemon from Oakland in a deal involving veteran Stan Bahnsen.

Those deals helped form the core of the South Side Hitmen, as the Sox slugged 192 home runs in '77, were in first place through August 19, and challenged Kansas City until the final three weeks of the season.

With the free-agent frenzy giving players a chance for freedom and greater riches, the short-pocketed Sox found themselves without a nucleus to build around. Resources would not return to a competitive level until Veeck sold the team to a group led by Reinsdorf and Eddie Einhorn in 1981. That enabled Hemond to make trades as well as introduce young players to the major leagues.

Hoyt and Richard Dotson, acquired in a trade from the Angels in 1978, anchored a deep pitching staff. Hemond added more speed with second baseman Julio Cruz to complement Rudy Law in center field. In 1983, the Sox won their first division title since Major League Baseball went to a four-division format in 1969 and made their first postseason appearance since 1959.

The '83 season brought greater expectations that the Sox failed to fulfill in two subsequent seasons, and Hemond was reassigned within the organization before taking over similar duties in Baltimore in 1987 and eventually returning to the Sox in an advisory capacity to Kenny Williams after the 2000 season.

Although Hemond now works for the Diamondbacks as an adviser, his legacy with the White Sox lives on with the Roland Hemond Award, instituted in 2003 to honor people committed to improving the lives of those around them, which parallels Hemond's all-around service to the game.

KEN "HAWK" HARRELSON (1985–86)

It's not uncommon for a manager to clash with a new general manager, but the landscape was lumpy before Ken "Hawk" Harrelson took over as the White Sox's general manager immediately after the 1985 season.

As a nine-year veteran slugger whose career was stunted by an ankle injury one year after being traded from Boston (where he still has a cult following) to Cleveland, Harrelson knew the often-cold realities of baseball. He conveyed them as an announcer with the Red Sox before joining the White Sox in a similar role from 1982 to 1985. But he had never worked in the front office.

Harrelson witnessed the White Sox's mini-zenith in 1983 as well as the unfulfilled expectations in 1984–85. Harrelson's plan convinced Reinsdorf enough to offer the GM job to him, which Harrelson stunningly accepted out of loyalty to his boss.

That plan included significant changes in player development and more specialization of instruction.

Harrelson's first move was hiring Alvin Dark as his farm director. Harrelson played for Dark with the Kansas City Athletics, but Dark gained greater success by taking San Francisco to its first World Series in 1962 and managing the Oakland Athletics to their third consecutive world championship in 1974.

The victim of Dark's hiring was David Dombrowski, an Oak Lawn native who was one of Hemond's most trusted assistants and would achieve greater success as GM in Montreal, Florida, and Detroit.

LOCAL BOY MAKES GOOD—ELSEWHERE

Oak Lawn native David Dombrowski always had ambitions for becoming a general manger. Dombrowski wrote a 63-page paper in October 1978 while a student at Western Michigan University titled "The General Manager: The Man in the Middle."

He interviewed 22 people and mailed questionnaires to several baseball executives. One of his meetings was an interview with White Sox GM Roland Hemond.

Hemond and baseball legend Paul Richards were so impressed with Dombrowski's upbeat attitude and eagerness that they brought him to the Comiskey Park offices. Dombrowski was hired as an administrative assistant and enrolled in night classes to fulfill his degree work.

Within 18 months, Dombrowski became the assistant director of player personnel. At the same time, he maximized his resources by picking the brains of manager Tony La Russa and later, coach Jim Leyland.

An average day for Dombrowski consisted of getting to the office at 9:00 AM and not leaving until 2:00 AM, as his duties included the smallest things, such as checking box scores in the paper so Hemond could determine if a player was hurt or not playing in case of a potential trade.

In 1981, Hemond convinced new bosses Jerry Reinsdorf and Eddie Einhorn that Dombrowski was ready to be the assistant GM at the tender age of 25. Dombrowski learned to speak Spanish at the suggestion of Hemond so he could prepare for the coming international influence in baseball, a theory he had documented in his college paper.

But Dombrowski was replaced by Alvin Dark in overseeing the farm system after Ken "Hawk" Harrelson took over as GM in 1986. Dombrowski quickly landed a job with the Montreal Expos and learned to speak French.

Dombrowski was Florida's first GM in 1992 and hired Leyland as manager to direct the Marlins to the 1997 World Series title. He would make a similar move in Detroit four years after taking over as team president, and the Tigers advanced to the 2006 World Series as a wild-card entrant.

"He doesn't forget the grass roots of the game," Hemond told the *Chicago Tribune* prior to the 2006 World Series. "He'll read what the computer says, but he'll always listen to his scouts."

Before manager Tony La Russa stepped onto the field for his seventh spring training with the White Sox, Harrelson changed the roster by dealing infielder Scott Fletcher and much-hyped pitching prospect Ed Correa to Texas for Wayne Tolleson and Dave Schmidt.

Fletcher, a popular member of the Winning Ugly team, became expendable with the emergence of 1985 Rookie of the Year Ozzie Guillen. Harrelson also dealt left-hander Britt Burns to New York, where he never pitched for the Yankees because of hip problems. Coming back to the Sox in the five-player trade was pitcher Joe Cowley, who won 11 games and hurled a no-hitter.

Days before the start of spring training, catcher Scott Bradley was acquired in another multiplayer deal with the Yankees. The move seemed minor until Bradley was traded at midseason for outfielder Ivan Calderon, who became a productive player with the White Sox.

The latter move came after Harrelson fired La Russa, who started 7–18 under the new GM in 1986 and was 26–38 with a sixth-place team at the time of his dismissal.

Eight years later, Reinsdorf called the firing a "great tragedy."

On the 20-year anniversary of his firing, La Russa said the partnership between himself and Harrelson was "unworkable."

The firing overshadowed Harrelson's attempts to retool the organization in the midst of a fifth-place season. La Russa, who was heavily booed toward the end of his White Sox tenure, was hired quickly by Oakland and took the Athletics to the World Series two seasons later.

Ken Harrelson's one-year tenure as White Sox GM is most remembered for his firing of manager Tony La Russa.

After La Russa's firing, Harrelson kept stitching the roster together, dealing Tom Seaver to Boston for utility player Steve Lyons, trading Bobby Bonilla back to Pittsburgh for pitcher Jose DeLeon (after drafting Bonilla in the Rule V Draft), and signing Steve Carlton and George Foster.

But worn down by a tumultuous first year in which he attempted to rebuild the organization, Harrelson resigned and retreated to the announcer's booth—with the New York Yankees—for two seasons before rejoining the White Sox's booth in 1990.

LARRY HIMES (1986-90)

Himes, who was a catcher at the University of Southern California under the late, great Rod Dedeaux, and was an assistant to coaching legend Augie Garrido at Cal Poly San Luis Obispo, believed firmly in structure.

After taking over as the White Sox's third GM in as many years, Himes stressed the need for continuity in management and believed that philosophy applied to more than just professional sports. Himes also emphasized implementing a plan and sticking with it; otherwise the plan would lose its effectiveness or be vulnerable to another change.

Himes interviewed seven candidates before hiring Jeff Torborg as manager. Himes felt Torborg was in line with his thinking and that of player development director Al Goldis.

The biggest accomplishments of the Himes era were his keen eye for amateur talent and not striking out on first-round picks.

An emphasis was placed on the amateur draft and a concentration on pitching, speed, and defense while recognizing that developing hitters was the toughest task in professional sports.

The Sox struck gold in four consecutive years with their first-round picks from 1987 to 1990—Stanford pitcher Jack McDowell, Oklahoma State third baseman Robin Ventura, Auburn first baseman Frank Thomas, and Miami-Dade Community College pitcher Alex Fernandez.

But as solid as Himes was in restructuring the farm system through the draft, he irritated enough important people to hasten his departure while in the midst of the Sox's 94-win season in 1990.

That was revealed by chairman Jerry Reinsdorf during an interview with longtime radio talk-show host Chet Coppock.

"The fact is, Larry Himes cannot get along with anybody," Reinsdorf told Coppock. "You can hardly find anybody in the Sox organization that wasn't happy when Larry Himes left."

Eighteen years later, Coppock still shakes his head at the candidness of Reinsdorf's comments about Himes.

"Reinsdorf was whupping him," Coppock recalled. "I think Reinsdorf had a tough time trying to figure out what Larry Himes was all about because Himes obviously hated the political side of baseball. Himes looked at the White Sox with Reinsdorf and the massive ownership group, and it drove him nuts because a lot of these guys thought they knew everything about baseball. Larry would be far more comfortable going over to UIC and looking at a junior left-hander from Youngstown State in the second game of a doubleheader."

Coppock believed Himes was a baseball purist who didn't like being second-guessed or questioned by those he believed lacked the knowledge to challenge him.

"I just think he was a brilliant talent evaluator who cost himself a lot of dough because he just couldn't and wouldn't play 'the game' because, to him, he was so far above the game that it was a personal insult of him to sit there and deal with Jerry or Lee Stern or Gene Fanning," Coppock said. "The ownership group would ask questions, and Larry would try to be cordial, but Larry's way of thinking was, 'You're an idiot. You're wasting my time.' So as a result, I think it got under Reinsdorf's skin, and Jerry has always liked guys who are very noteworthy—Ozzie, La Russa, Hawk.

"Hawk will tell you in 1986 that he did a rotten job as GM, but Jerry never gave up on Hawk. Jerry likes people that he figures he can sip Scotch with or smoke a cigar with. And that was the last guy in the world that Himes was going to be."

The dismissal of Himes baffles Coppock, to some extent, because the media climate wasn't nearly as intense as it is now.

"He frustrated the people around him because he wasn't a great communicator, but he wasn't a bad guy by any sense of the imagination," Coppock said. "He was very cordial. He would return calls. He was available. But I didn't think I knew Larry better in year four than day one.

"It's a tougher media now, but in 1990, I've always maintained that anybody who thought Chicago was a tough media town is crazy because it's the softest big-city media town in America. All you have to do is just answer a couple phone calls and play the game and everything would be fine.

"But Larry was too busy worrying about a third baseman at Arizona State to ever get involved in politics."

Himes also rattled some of his players by fining them if they didn't wear socks, and he banned alcohol in the clubhouse and on charter flights.

"Why invite trouble?" Coppock asked. "Why invite a bunch of brats for no good darn reason? Larry, this isn't the U.S. Marines. We're not guards at Guantanamo Bay. We're not worrying about the security of the Oval Office. I remember [Steve] Rainbow Trout showing up for a pitching assignment in 1982 with his shirt cut down to his navel and saying, 'Who are we playing?'

"[Himes] would do little annoying things like that. It was like he was trying to have a perfect baseball world where everyone would wear Brooks Brothers suits and socks. Nobody would wear jeans or think of having a beer from Chicago to Seattle. And all the players would be responsive.

"One thing he didn't care about was if the players liked him or not. He didn't care if anyone liked him or not. He didn't have time for it."

But not all the players balked at all of Himes' mandates.

"Those are rules," said Ozzie Guillen, who was in his sixth season as a player and respected Himes' structure. "That's the way it should be. Your boss is your boss, no matter what you do. If you don't [like it], [bleep] it. I don't know why people were concerned about it. Larry wanted to represent our organization the right way. I don't have any problem with Larry.

"The only problem I had with Larry was no alcohol in the clubhouse. Come on, that's immature. We don't have juvenile kids here. But that's the only problem I have with him."

Himes remains an enigma to those around the White Sox.

"I think people don't appreciate what Larry did because of the way he was," Guillen said. "He and Al Goldis were lucky. They had their opportunity to pick the right people, and they picked their own guys. You have to be lucky or have good scouting."

Coppock had difficulty reading Himes' emotions.

"I don't know to this day if you could call him a happy man or unhappy man. I haven't seen Larry in years. I can only assume he's happy, and the reason I think he is happy is that he feels, 'This is my world. I can find my world,'" Coppock said.

Despite the sour end to Himes' regime, he still had his boosters who appreciated his support and interest in player development through the draft.

"Let me tell you something," said Phil Rizzo, a former White Sox scout. "I love Al Goldis. Even Mike [Phil's son, who scouted Frank Thomas] and I, there's nothing we wouldn't do for Al Goldis and even Larry Himes. I know they have their good things and their bad things, but these two guys were very good to the Rizzos. When you're good to us, you know there's nothing we wouldn't do for you.

"One thing we don't do—we don't b.s. one another."

RON SCHUELER (1990–2000)

As a large man who looked most comfortable in cowboy boots than penny loafers, Ron Schueler fit the profile of a throwback talent evaluator.

A cell phone or Blackberry wouldn't look right attached to this former pitcher who lasted eight years in the majors with four teams before concluding his career with the White Sox.

In fact, Schueler was a pitching coach with the Sox, A's, and Pirates before joining the Athletics' front office as a professional and amateur scout.

That diverse background helped him when he took over the Sox. His initial mission was to acquire complementary players to fortify a seasoned team, before shifting his focus to the farm system.

On Schueler's plus side, the Sox finished first or second in their division in eight of the 10 seasons he served as GM. But only two of those were division titles (in 1993 and 2000). The Sox posted the fourth-best record (817–734) during Schueler's reign, but never won a league championship.

Despite a knack for bringing in talent—including Bo Jackson and Tim Raines in 1991, Ellis Burks in 1993, and Albert Belle in 1997—the infamous "White Flag Trade" in 1997 will always cloud Schueler's place in Sox lore.

San Francisco, trying to cling onto first place in the National League West and hold off a wealthier and more talented Los Angeles Dodgers team, looked to the Sox as a team that could provide help for its struggling bullpen. Once the Giants knew they could acquire Roberto Hernandez to aid Rod Beck, they probed Schueler about the availability of left-hander Wilson Alvarez and versatile Danny Darwin.

Former Sox pitcher Dick Tidrow, the Giants' chief talent evaluator, spent more than a week watching the Sox and served as GM Brian Sabean's front man.

The White Sox ended up receiving six young players of varying talents—pitchers Keith Foulke, Bob Howry, Lorenzo Barcelo, and Ken Vining, shortstop Mike Caruso, and outfielder Brian Manning—but the blockbuster deal ended any chance they had of earning a postseason berth. And of the six players they acquired, none reached All-Star status while playing for the White Sox.

For better or worse, GM Ron Schueler is most remembered for engineering the White Flag Trade in 1997.

Schueler stepped down as GM in 2000, and a telling scene between Schueler and his successors occurred before a 2007 Cactus League game involving the White Sox and A's at Phoenix Municipal Stadium in the media dining area. Schueler sat at one table with two reporters, while at least four Sox staff members sat at an adjacent table and barely made eye contact with him. Finally, Scott Reifert, the Sox's mild-mannered vice president of communications, extended a handshake and had a friendly discussion with Schueler, who was serving as a special assistant to the St. Louis Cardinals.

Ironically, it was Schueler's recruiting skills and knowledge that helped San Francisco, his current employer, land former Sox fan favorite Aaron Rowand at the cost of five years and $60 million. The Sox weren't willing to give Rowand a fifth season.

KENNY WILLIAMS (2000-PRESENT)

Kenny Williams and Billy Beane are two of only three active GMs who played in the major leagues. The similarities don't end there.

Both were relative failures as players, but have attained different degrees of success as executives with varying methods.

Overseeing a large-market team in a heavily scrutinized market, Williams has worked with greater resources to obtain what Beane hasn't achieved—a World Series title.

But Beane has won more division titles with fewer resources to the admiration of media outlets across the nation. Despite putting together a White Sox team that won the franchise's first World Series in 88 years, Williams didn't win the Executive of the Year Award in 2005. That honor went to Cleveland's Mark Shapiro despite the fact that the Indians didn't make the playoffs following a strong second-half push.

Ironically, Williams and Beane love to trade and have done so several times with one another. Many of the deals could be considered minor, with the exception of Williams acquiring switch-hitting center fielder/first baseman Nick Swisher for three prospects in 2008. (Swisher was then dealt to the Yankees after his one season in Chicago.)

That deal fits the image of both teams and their top baseball evaluators: Williams aiming sky-high for a championship each year while Beane looks to the distant future by trading for cheap but celebrated talent.

The expectations are greater for Williams, and he's not shy about reaching to meet them. Less than a month after winning the World Series in 2005, Williams traded center fielder and fan favorite Aaron Rowand to land designated hitter Jim Thome in hopes of winning a second consecutive World Series title.

Williams' favorite football team is the Oakland Raiders, led by maverick managing general partner Al Davis. Williams has adopted Davis' trait of acquiring players who failed to reach their potential in other organizations. For example, Williams traded for controversial switch-hitting slugger Carl Everett on two different occasions, and Everett helped push the Sox to victory in '05.

Kenny Williams has brought a win-at-all-costs mentality to the White Sox front office since being named GM in 2000. Photo courtesy of AP Images.

Williams also dealt All-Star pitcher Esteban Loaiza around the 2004 trading deadline for pitcher Jose Contreras, who didn't develop as quickly as the New York Yankees hoped after signing him to a four-year, $32 million contract shortly following his defection from Cuba.

Williams' vision became somewhat broader after landing All-Star pitchers David Wells and Bartolo Colon early in his tenure, only to fall short of landing a postseason berth.

Williams relied on videotapes as much as scouting reports when he signed second baseman Tadahito Iguchi before the 2005 season. He has gradually delegated more talent evaluating duties to vice president/assistant GM Rick Hahn—who is well polished in contract negotiations and has interviewed for several GM positions—and Dan Fabian—the Sox director of baseball operations who started his career as an intern in the team's public relations department.

After his lackluster playing career ended, Williams returned to the Sox to become the director of minor league operations for two seasons before being promoted to vice president of player development (1997–2000).

Although Williams has a deep stable of seasoned professional scouts, he's not afraid to step in and take charge. For example, Joe Butler and Gary Pellant spent several miserable summer nights in Tucson watching Carlos Quentin, Arizona's injury-prone young outfielder, but Williams says he was more convinced than his scouts that Quentin would blossom into a productive player and was worth the price of trading lower-level first base slugger Chris Carter.

"If I can point to one thing that I'm strongest at in this position, it's scouting," Williams said in late April when Quentin began his ascent. "And I have my own ideas. While I certainly factor in the scouting reports, I'm my own advocate."

No trade illustrated Williams' confidence and trust in his own evaluation more than a stunning deadline deal in 2008 that brought storied slugger Ken Griffey Jr. to the Sox in exchange for middle reliever Nick Masset and infielder Danny Richar.

It seemed like Williams had coveted Griffey dating back to at least 2005, when Williams pursued the slugger even though the Sox seemed well equipped in the outfield with speedy Scott Podsednik in left field, Jermaine Dye in right field, and fan-favorite and gritty Aaron Rowand in center field. The trade never took place, as Reds ownership balked at picking up a large sum of the balance of Griffey's contract.

That wasn't the case in 2008, as the Sox only had to pay a pro-rated portion of the minimum salary of $390,000 left on Griffey's $12.5 million salary for 2008, and the Sox and Reds agreed to split the balance of his $4 million buyout for 2009.

This deal displayed Williams' determination to get a deal done, no matter how little time he had to work with. After trying desperately to land a reliever while waiting for Paul Konerko and Nick Swisher to break out of their slumps, Williams shifted gears with less than 30 hours left before the non-waiver trading deadline.

Cincinnati GM Walt Jocketty said in a telephone conference call that Williams first inquired about Griffey early in the afternoon of July 30. Because Williams respects Jocketty's evaluations and negotiating skills, the two sides quickly agreed on compensation, with approval later from their ownership groups on how the balance of Griffey's contract would be settled.

After Griffey completed his game at Houston, he was summoned into an office to accept a trade to the Sox. He then ate his postgame meal before boarding a plane to Washington, D.C.

When Fox Sports' Ken Rosenthal broke the story the following morning, none of the Sox's top professional scouts were aware of what Williams had worked on and accomplished in less than 24 hours.

Although Griffey didn't make a huge contribution in his first and only season with the Sox, his acquisition did give the Sox needed depth after Quentin was lost for the final four weeks of the season because of a broken right wrist.

HALL OF FAMERS, ALL-STARS, AND BIG NAMES

HALL OF FAMERS

The White Sox are represented in Cooperstown by 26 former players, managers, and executives. But only 11 of those 26 spent the majority of their careers in the White Sox organization.

Ed Walsh (1904–16)

A look at 1908 represents one of the greatest seasons by a pitcher—ever. Walsh was 40–15 with a 1.42 ERA in 66 games, 49 of them starts.

That added up to an astonishing 464 innings, one season after Walsh threw 422⅓ innings while posting a 24–18 record.

Walsh's career was enhanced, strangely enough, by learning the spitball, which wasn't ruled illegal until 1920.

Walsh threw the first no-hitter at Comiskey Park on August 27, 1911, against Boston. Walsh threw 393 innings the following season before he began to wear down and become less effective.

Nevertheless, he won 24 games or more in a season four times, which helped him get inducted into the Hall in 1946. Walsh later served as a coach and was an interim manager for three games in 1924.

Ray Schalk (1912–28)

Schalk was the Pudge Rodriguez of his day. At 5'9" and 165 pounds, Schalk was one of the best defensive catchers of his era, although he batted only .254 in 17 seasons with the White Sox and hit only 11 home runs during that span.

Schalk played in 123 games or more 11 times during a 13-season stretch. He led American League catchers in fielding five times and caught four no-hitters.

Unfortunately for the Sox and Schalk, he was appointed as manager but lasted only one and a half seasons before resigning midway through the 1928 season.

Nevertheless, he was inducted into the Hall in 1955.

Red Faber (1914–33)

Faber, whose actual first name was Urban, came to the White Sox from the Pittsburgh organization but was courted by the New York Giants during the World Tour before throwing a pitch in Chicago. Faber impressed Giants manager John McGraw, but McGraw couldn't persuade White Sox owner Charles Comiskey to sell him.

Faber proved his worth immediately by posting a 2.68 ERA in his first season with the Sox, and then winning 24 games the following season.

Faber didn't pitch in the 1919 Black Sox World Series because of illness, but he rebounded the next three years with 69 victories.

Faber was inducted into the Hall in 1964.

Eddie Collins (1915–26)

Collins started and ended his baseball career with the Philadelphia Athletics, but he made a great impression in a White Sox uniform.

Ten times Collins batted over .300, including a .372 mark in 1920 when he was 33 years old. As a left-handed-hitting second baseman, Collins had greater ambitions.

He became a player-manager for the White Sox during his final two seasons and directed them to two winning seasons before being fired.

Collins returned to Philadelphia as a player-coach and was inducted into the Hall in 1939.

Second baseman Eddie Collins played 12 seasons for the White Sox and retired with 3,315 career hits.

Ted Lyons (1923–42, 1946)

Lyons was elected to the Hall in 1955, nine seasons after completing a career in which he won 260 games and led the American League with 21 wins in 1925 and 22 in 1927.

Lyons succeeded despite pitching on losing teams in 14 of his 21 seasons. The development of a knuckleball enhanced his longevity.

Lyons managed the Sox from 1946 to 1948 and later became a scout who signed outfielder Ken Berry and pitcher Joel Horlen. His No. 16 was retired in 1987.

Luke Appling (1930–43, 1945–50)

One of the greatest deals of the Comiskey era was trading out-fielder Douglas Taitt and $20,000 to the Cubs for Appling, one of the greatest hitters in White Sox history.

Appling was voted into the Hall in 1964. He is the White Sox's career leader in games (2,422), at-bats (8,857), and hits (2,749), and is second in doubles (440), runs (1,319), walks (1,302), triples (102), and RBIs (1,116).

Appling's No. 4 jersey was retired in 1975. He also served as a coach with the White Sox in 1970–71.

One of Appling's greatest feats occurred after his playing days ended. In 1982, the 75-year-old Appling hit a home run out of RFK Stadium in Washington, D.C., off Warren Spahn in an old timers' game.

Nellie Fox (1950–63)

Perhaps no White Sox player got more out of his talent than the 5'9", 160-pound Fox. He batted over .300 six times during his first 10 seasons with the Sox.

Fox was elected to the Hall in 1997 after 14 seasons with the White Sox. A 12-time American League All-Star, Fox was the league's MVP during the White Sox's AL title season in 1959.

Fox led the league in hits in 1952, 1954, 1957, and 1958. He also earned three AL Gold Glove Awards for his solid defense at

Nellie Fox was the American League MVP in 1959 and led the Sox to the World Series.

second base. In 1958, Fox played 98 consecutive games without striking out.

His No. 2 was retired in 1976.

Luis Aparicio (1956–62, 1968–70)

Aparicio teamed with Fox to form one of the best double-play combinations in baseball. Aparicio followed fellow Venezuelan Chico Carrasquel at shortstop for the White Sox, and his defense and speed made him an instant hit with fans. Aparicio stole 160 bases from 1959 to 1961 and remained a very durable and productive player despite the demands of his position.

As productive and as valuable as Aparicio was, GM Ed Short dealt him to Baltimore before the 1963 season, and Aparacio didn't return to the White Sox until 1968.

As a 35-year-old, Aparacio stole 24 bases for the White Sox and batted .313 in 146 games in 1970—his final season in Chicago before heading to Boston.

Aparicio was voted to the Hall in 1984. He was a nine-time Gold Glove Award winner as a slick-fielding shortstop and was named to the AL All-Star team 10 times. Aparicio was the AL Rookie of the Year in 1956.

Al Lopez (1957–65, 1968–69)

Until 2005, Al Lopez had the distinction of being the last manager to direct the White Sox to the World Series. He also gained popularity among haters of New York City by snatching the American League pennant away from the Yankees during their impressive run, previously accomplishing the feat with the 1954 Cleveland Indians that featured Hall of Fame pitchers Early Wynn, Bob Feller, and Bob Lemon, and tough-minded third baseman Al Rosen.

Lopez managed nine consecutive winning seasons (1957–65) and was known for his faith in his players, although the 1959 pennant was as good as it got for a team traditionally frustrated by the Yankees' dominance.

Lopez returned to manage briefly in 1968 and 1969 before retiring for good. He passed away days after the White Sox won the 2005 World Series.

Carlton Fisk (1981–93)

The aggressiveness of new owners, led by Jerry Reinsdorf and Eddie Einhorn, shocked many baseball followers after the Sox snagged Fisk away from Boston via free agency in 1981.

Fisk immediately gave his new bosses a quick return by hitting a game-winning home run at Fenway Park, and he survived 12 seasons battling front-office officials before his release midway through the 1993 season.

One of the most enigmatic characters in White Sox history, Fisk was notorious for slowing down games and talking to pitchers, as well as working out endlessly after games.

The hard work paid off, as Fisk caught 2,226 games and was behind the plate in 106 games in 1991 at the age of 43. He played 31 games in left field during the turbulent 1986 season but returned to full-time status behind the plate the following season.

Four of Fisk's 11 All-Star selections came with the White Sox, as well as all three Silver Slugger Awards for his offensive production at his position.

Fisk was voted into the Hall in 2000, and a statue of Fisk at U.S. Cellular Field was unveiled in 2005. He also agreed to rejoin the Sox in a special assistant capacity in 2008.

Though Carlton Fisk entered the National Baseball Hall of Fame wearing a Red Sox cap, he remains beloved by White Sox fans.

Charles Comiskey (1900–31)

Comiskey was selected to the Hall of Fame by the Veterans Committee in 1939—20 years after the Black Sox Scandal in which players were found to have thrown the World Series partly because of Comiskey's frugal treatment of them.

Although Comiskey was selected to the Hall as an executive, he played 13 seasons and is credited with revolutionizing the position of first base. He also served as manager for 12 of those seasons with three teams in the American Association, Players League, and National League before shifting to management, and helped move his St. Paul minor league team to Chicago, where it became a member of the new American League.

ALL-STARS

Harold Baines

On July 22, 2007, the White Sox unveiled a bronze statue of Harold Baines, one of the team's greatest hitters and perhaps the most controversial-free player in franchise history.

The statue accurately depicts Baines, with his signature right-leg kick that helped generate his signature left-handed swing.

For Baines, the statue represents the White Sox's appreciation for his greatness that covered three stints (1980–89, 1996–97, and 2000–01) over 14 big-league seasons. The recognition of Baines' accomplishments with the Sox is typified by the fact that his No. 3 jersey was retired by the White Sox in 1989—less than halfway through his remarkable career.

But baseball's highest honor still eludes Baines, currently a first-base coach with the White Sox. After learning that third baseman Ron Santo, who played the 1974 season with the White Sox but batted just .221 and questioned Dick Allen's special privileges, believed having his number retired by the Cubs was better than being elected to the Hall of Fame, the statue has become a worthy consolation prize for Baines.

"I'd be lying if I said I didn't want to be in the Hall of Fame," Baines said shortly before ceremonies unveiling his statue on the concourse at U.S. Cellular Field. "This is a great honor, too. When an organization is going to put a statue up in their stadium forever...[Santo] might be right. That's better than the Hall of Fame to me. That shows my family and me that we represented the White Sox well."

How well?

Baines was a six-time All-Star, batted .300 or higher eight times, and produced 11 seasons with 20 or more home runs. He also backed up his reputation as one of baseball's greatest clutch hitters with a .324 batting average with five home runs and 16 RBIs in 31 postseason games.

But Baines received only 5.3 percent of the vote for the National Baseball Hall of Fame in 2007, barely making him eligible for the 2008 ballot. For automatic induction into the Hall, a player must receive at least 75 percent of the votes cast by the Baseball Writers Association of America voters (who all must have at least 10 years of BBWAA service).

Each candidate (who must have played at least 10 seasons and have been retired for at least five years before his election) is judged by his record, playing ability, integrity, sportsmanship, character, and contributions to the teams he played with.

In addition to his hitting prowess, Baines possessed a powerful arm and collected 24 assists in 1985 and 1986. Unfortunately,

Harold Baines was a cornerstone of the White Sox throughout the 1980s.

bad knees relegated Baines to designated-hitter duty for the bulk of his career.

But that didn't limit his hitting ability. Baines won the 1989 American League Silver Slugger Award by hitting .309 with 16 home runs and 72 RBIs with the Sox and Texas Rangers. He also proved to be a beacon of consistency with 1,628 RBIs despite driving in 100 runs or more in only three seasons (1982, 1985, 1999).

While there's little doubt that Baines carried himself with class and without drawing attention to himself, the fact that he played a majority of his games as a DH has penalized his chances.

Paul Molitor, who, like Baines, played a majority of his games as a DH (1,174), was inducted into the Hall of Fame in 2004 with 85.2 percent of the ballots cast. Molitor, however, collected 3,319 hits to Baines' 2,866.

Tim Raines

Harold Baines barely stayed on the 2009 Hall of Fame ballot after being named on 5.2 percent of the ballots in 2008.

The debate is even more intriguing for Tim Raines, who was named on 24.3 percent of the ballots in his first year of eligibility in 2008.

Most of Raines' accomplishments occurred with the Montreal Expos, where he quickly developed a reputation as one of top leadoff hitters in the game. He continued his success following a trade to the White Sox in December 1990, although the statistics weren't nearly as impressive as they were during his first 12 seasons with the Expos.

In Montreal, Raines was a National League All-Star for seven consecutive seasons (1981–87), a four-time NL stolen-base champion, and won the 1986 NL batting title. His 1987 season ranks as one of the most remarkable (.309 batting average and 50 stolen bases) because, thanks to the owners' collusion that illegally attempted to keep players' salaries down and prevented Raines from negotiating with Montreal until May 1, he was limited to just 139 games. He still holds the highest stolen-base percentage (.857) of any player with at least 300 attempts.

With the White Sox, Raines stole 143 bases in five seasons, including 51 in 1991. He was one of the key players on the White Sox's 1993 American League West title team, hitting .306 with 16 home runs and 21 stolen bases.

Raines set an AL record with 40 consecutive stolen bases without getting caught that started at the end of the 1993 season and continued until September 2, 1995—two weeks short of his 36th birthday. Raines didn't win his first World Series until he was traded the following year to the New York Yankees.

Raines was second to all-time base-stealing leader Rickey Henderson among the top leadoff batters of the 1980s, and Raines' 808 stolen bases rank a firm fifth on the career list.

But Raines' legacy might have been negatively impacted by his longevity. He played 23 seasons, but his role diminished in the final years as a huge emphasis on power swelled throughout the majors.

Raines sought treatment for a cocaine addiction after the 1982 season but never caused any problems with his teammates. In fact, Paul Molitor was inducted into the Hall well after admitting to a drug addiction during his playing days.

Roberto Alomar

General manager Kenny Williams thought so much of Alomar that he acquired him *twice* near the end of his storied career.

Unfortunately for Alomar and the Sox his best days were behind him, but his best moments should be enough for a Hall of Fame induction.

Alomar batted .253 in 67 games with the Sox after coming over in a trade from the New York Mets in 2003. He returned for the final two months of the 2004 season after being plagued by injuries in Arizona but batted only .180 in 61 at-bats.

Alomar's production prior to joining the White Sox made him one of the top players ever to play the position, placing him alongside Hall of Famers Ryne Sandberg and Joe Morgan.

Alomar was a 10-time Gold Glove second baseman who was named to 12 All-Star teams and earned four Silver Slugger Awards for his offensive production at second base. Like White Sox manager Ozzie Guillen, Alomar started his career with San Diego, but his career blossomed after moving to the American League with Toronto, Baltimore, and Cleveland.

His detractors will point to the fact that he played in three hitter-friendly parks (Rogers Centre, Oriole Park, and Jacobs Field), but Alomar batted .300 or better in six consecutive seasons and nine of 10 with the Blue Jays, Indians, and Orioles.

In the AL MVP balloting, Alomar finished third in 1999 and fourth in 2001. His consistency was impressive, although he never won a batting title or led the league in stolen bases, and he did not retire with more than 3,000 hits.

Part of Alomar's legacy is tarnished by an incident on September 27, 1996, in which he spit at umpire John Hirschbeck during an argument at home plate. That ugly outburst caused him to be suspended for five games, but he and Hirschbeck later made their peace.

But with the White Sox, Alomar was just another fading star who was unsuccessful in getting to the postseason.

Jim Thome

Before coming to the White Sox after the 2005 season, Jim Thome had played in only 59 games in 2004 because of a lower back strain and right elbow surgery.

Under pressure to help the White Sox defend their 2005 World Series title and being the centerpiece of a trade that saw fan favorite Aaron Rowand dealt to Philadelphia, Thome rebounded with 42 home runs, 109 RBIs, and a .288 batting average.

Despite becoming a full-time designated hitter, Thome's power hasn't tailed off despite playing in an era more scrutinized by drug testing. He has hit 30 or more home runs in 12 of his last 13 seasons, including 42 or more in four straight years (2001–04).

Since joining the White Sox, Thome has climbed past the likes of Hall of Famers Mickey Mantle, Jimmie Foxx, Ted Williams, and Willie McCovey on the all-time home-run list.

Like Williams and McCovey, Thome has coped with an exaggerated shift in which opponents place three defenders to the right of second base in an attempt to cut off Thome's hard line

Since joining the Sox in 2006, Jim Thome has climbed to 14th on the all-time home-run list. Photo courtesy of AP Images.

drives. But after a slow start in 2008, Thome learned to hit to the opposite field with more success, and his production helped kick-start the White Sox's offense and kept them in first place throughout most of the season.

Thome's skeptics point to the fact that he has never won an MVP Award and led the league in home runs only once. They also note that Thome wasn't the best fielder, as evidenced by his shift from third base to first to make room for Gold Glove third baseman Matt Williams before the 1997 season with Cleveland, and then by becoming a full-time DH after joining the White Sox.

But in addition to his power, Thome has ranked in the top six in on-base percentage in nine seasons, thus creating scoring opportunities for his teammates.

One of his most memorable moments occurred with the White Sox on September 16, 2007, when he hit a walk-off home run off the Los Angeles Angels' Dustin Moseley for his 500th career blast.

It also was Jim Thome Bobblehead Doll day, so fans had plenty to remember. And after several weather-induced postponements,

Thome was able to personally deliver the ball to Hall of Fame officials in Cooperstown on August 28, 2008.

Thome could be making another visit in the future.

BIG NAMES

The White Sox collected their share of All-Stars and Hall of Famers past their prime well before Kenny Williams pulled off the deadline acquisition of Ken Griffey Jr. in 2008.

There have been various reasons for these trades, but they've each gained their share of notoriety.

Ted Kluszewski

The White Sox acquired Kluszewski in a trade from Pittsburgh in late August of 1959 while in the heat of an American League pennant race with Cleveland.

It was clear that Kluszewski's best days were behind him, as he hit only two home runs in 60 games before the Pirates sent him to the Sox. This was a significant drop-off from his stretch of 171 home runs from 1953 to 1956 with Cincinnati, where Kluszewski looked more intimidating in a sleeveless jersey.

Kluszewski hit his only two home runs of the regular season on September 7 against Kansas City in the second game of a doubleheader. He batted .297 with only 10 RBIs in 31 regular-season games for the Sox, but he became an instant hero in Game 1 of the 1959 World Series when he duplicated his two-home-run, five-RBI performance in an 11–0 win over the Los Angeles Dodgers.

Kluszewski finished the six-game series with a .391 batting average, three home runs, and 10 RBIs. He hit only five home runs in 81 games the following season, however, and was left unprotected and was claimed by the Los Angeles Angels in the 1961 expansion draft.

Bobby Bonds

Bonds' stint with the Sox was so short, he's mostly remembered as the "other" player in the six-player deal that brought pitcher Richard Dotson and outfielder Thad Bosley from California.

In 1977, the 32-year-old Bonds hit 37 home runs, drove in 115 runs, and stole 41 bases for the Angels. But in 26 games with the Sox in 1978, he batted just .278 with only two home runs in 90 at-bats before being shipped off to Texas for outfielders Claudell Washington and Rusty Torres.

The White Sox were the first of five teams that Bonds played for during the final four years of his talented but mercurial career.

Tom Seaver

In one of the more stunning developments in the history of free agency, the White Sox selected Seaver as a free-agent compensation pick in 1984. Seaver, 39, was coming off a 9–14 season and the Mets incorrectly anticipated that no one would select him.

Seaver ended up leading the White Sox's pitching staff in 1984 with 15 victories. The success was bittersweet because the team finished fifth just one year removed from their 1983 American League West title.

Seaver was even better in 1985, winning 16 games and lowering his ERA to 3.17. Although the dirt on his right knee from his leg drive in a Mets uniform is a signature photo, Seaver earned his

Hall of Famer Tom Seaver went 33–28 during parts of three seasons with the White Sox.

300th career victory in a Sox jersey on August 4 at Yankee Stadium on Phil Rizzuto Day.

But the White Sox slid from first place near midseason to third place. Seaver slumped to 2–6 during a turbulent 1986 season that saw Tony La Russa fired on June 20, and Seaver was dealt nine days later to Boston.

Steve Carlton

Less than a week after San Francisco released him and less than two months after Philadelphia—where he gained Hall of Fame success—dumped him after 14½ seasons, Carlton signed with the White Sox.

The signing came while the White Sox were concluding a 90-loss season in 1986. After lasting only three innings in his first start, Carlton, 38, actually pitched adequately with the White Sox. He pitched into the seventh inning in seven of his final nine starts and finished with a 4–3 record and a 3.69 ERA.

But with Hawk Harrelson leaving as GM and a new emphasis on youth under new GM Larry Himes, Carlton was not invited back for 1987. Nevertheless, he pitched parts of the next two seasons with Cleveland and Minnesota and finished with 329 victories.

Rob Dibble

In 1995, the White Sox took a chance on Dibble, a flame-throwing two-time National League All-Star who missed all of the 1994 season because of surgery. He actually started his stint with the White Sox in the minor leagues and was promoted despite posting a 7.86 ERA in eight games with Double-A Birmingham.

Dibble pitched in 16 games, but his control problems persisted. He walked 27 and uncorked five wild pitches in just 14½ innings. He did collect one save by striking out Chuck Knoblauch and inducing Rich Becker to pop to second to preserve Jason Bere's 4–3 win at Minnesota on June 28.

Dibble was released less than a month later by the White Sox and finished the final two months of the 1995 season with Milwaukee.

Jose Canseco

Since Kenny Williams took over as general manager after the 2000 season, he has been open-minded about giving players, coaches, and other staffers second chances.

That applied to Jose Canseco well before Canseco blew the whistle on baseball for its steroid problem.

Canseco managed to earn a World Series ring with the 2000 New York Yankees and had signed the following winter with the California Angels, only to be released after the Angels acquired Glenallen Hill from the Yankees shortly before the start of the 2001 season.

Canseco, sitting on 446 career home runs, was relegated to playing for Newark of the independent Atlantic League. He hit seven home runs with 27 RBIs in 41 games, which was enough for the Sox to purchase his contract and put him on the major league roster three weeks after the Angels released Hill.

Canseco hit 16 home runs with 49 RBIs in only 76 games for the Sox. He signed a free-agent contract with Montreal but was released before the 2002 season. The Sox re-signed him to a minor league contract but he played in only 18 games with Charlotte, hitting five homers before being released and later moving on to more controversial issues.

In his final big-league season, Jose Canseco hit 16 home runs in 76 games for the 2001 White Sox.
Photo courtesy of AP Images.

WINNING UGLY

"That was a special year," said Greg Walker, who had several reasons to remember the 1983 White Sox.

For general manger Roland Hemond and manager Tony La Russa, it was a year of satisfaction and redemption after receiving a groundswell of scrutiny and criticism for not finishing higher than third place since La Russa had taken over for Don Kessinger in the middle of the 1979 season.

The Sox incorporated a mix of youngsters including Ron Kittle and Walker with veterans like free-agent left-hander Floyd Bannister from Seattle. The addition of second baseman Julio Cruz from Seattle on June 15 added more speed to a lineup that included Rudy Law, whose 77 stolen bases remain a franchise record.

The Sox, who were in fifth place at the time of the Cruz trade, embarked on a 12–5 run to end the first half with a 40–37 record, and then embarked on a 59–26 run following the All-Star break to run away with their first division title.

It was particularly special for Walker, who had missed nearly all of 1982 because of a wrist injury and thought he wasn't going to make the Opening Day roster.

"Because of the injury, I didn't anticipate making the team," said Walker, who was 23 at the time. "They had two veteran first basemen, Tom Paciorek and Mike Squires. I went to spring training, but didn't have a good spring.

Jerry Reinsdorf, Tony La Russa, and Eddie Einhorn combined to guide the White Sox to the postseason in 1983.

"I got called into the office the day before we were breaking camp and I thought it was to be sent down, and Tony told me we'd be a better team if I was starting opening night in Texas.

"So I promptly went out and committed two errors."

For left-hander Kevin Hickey, who didn't play high school baseball and was signed at a tryout camp, the progression to being part of a division title team was like opening holiday gifts for three consecutive days.

"My first year was in 1981, and I was told I was going north with the team," said Hickey, now a batting-practice pitcher whom A.J. Pierzynski says could still pitch in the majors.

"We were in Bradenton, and I hurried to tell my family. I felt like Superman looking for the telephone booth," he said.

Hickey viewed his first two seasons as a preparation period for 1983.

"Night in and night out, and day in and day out, it was a different individual who came through for us," Hickey said. "We didn't depend on just one guy. It was both veterans and youngsters who came through."

Hickey roomed with reliever Dennis Lamp, who had learned how to stay loose and on an even keel with the help of Ed Farmer, a South Side native who pitched for the Sox from 1979 to 1981 and now serves as the Sox's play-by-play radio announcer.

"The funniest one was when Ed Farmer had the Mr. Spock ears, and he went down to the Boston bullpen and he put the ears on," Hickey recalled. "The only person who could outtalk Ed Farmer was Dennis Lamp. And in Kansas City, Lamp fell asleep in the bullpen and had his mouth wide open, and Farmer would take half a bag of Red Man [chewing tobacco] and shove it in his mouth and the bullpen phone would ring and they'd tell Lamp to get up and the next thing you know, he'd be gagging on Red Man.

"It kept you at ease, and the war stories you heard kept you loose. It was fun. I learned a lot."

The White Sox were swept in their opening series at Texas, but managed to hold strong through the leadership of La Russa and several seasoned veterans thirsting for a chance at the postseason.

"It was a tremendous group of veteran leaders, guys who had won before," Walker recalled. "Jerry Koosman, Carlton Fisk, Greg Luzinski, Tom Paciorek, and Dick Tidrow in the bullpen."

Kittle said that despite the array of experience on the roster, every player was treated equally.

"The funny thing is that you sometimes hear about other teams where they say, 'You're a rookie, you can't do this,'" Kittle said. "But everyone knew their place and how important they were. The younger guys picked up on what the veterans said and did, and the veterans fed off the youngsters' energy.

"There was not one single day I didn't want to be the hero."

La Russa, according to Walker, did a masterful job of keeping his players happy despite not being able to play all his veterans on a regular basis.

"We were winning," Walker said. "The pitching staff in the second half was phenomenal. That's what made that team very good. LaMarr Hoyt, Richard Dotson, and Floyd Bannister had phenomenal second halves. I think the turnaround offensively is when we traded for Julio Cruz to give us another speed guy, with Rudy Law, who could make things happen on the base paths. We also had some guys like Jerry Dybzinski, Scott Fletcher, and Vance Law who knew how to play the game. And we had power in the middle."

But the offense didn't start to generate runs until May 20, when La Russa moved Fisk up to second. Fisk, batting .173 at the time, went 2-for-5 with an RBI in a 9–6 win over Kansas City. The switch helped Fisk raise his batting average to .289 while giving emerging Harold Baines, Luzinski, Kittle, and Paciorek more opportunities to drive in runs.

Baines hit 20 home runs and drove in 99 runs, Luzinski smacked 32 homers and drove in 95 runs, and Kittle "took the league by storm," in the words of Walker, slugging 35 home runs and driving in 100—both team highs—to earn AL Rookie of the Year honors.

"But what made it special was the makeup and the veteran leadership," Walker said. "It kept a young team together—very close. Tony was very good at doing this."

And the White Sox got stronger as the skepticism over their

credentials increased. Before losing three of four at home to the White Sox in late August, Texas manager and future interim Sox boss Doug Rader provided the division leaders with some bulletin-board fodder.

"They're winning ugly," Rader told Randy Youngman of the now-defunct *Dallas Times Herald*. "At least that's what our reports say."

"Funny thing is, Doug Rader considered it an insult,"

Sweet-swinging first baseman Greg Walker hit .270 and knocked in 55 runs for the Sox in 1983.

Richard Justice, who wrote the "Winning Ugly" story, said 25 years later. "He thought he was putting the White Sox in their place. But the White Sox loved it, made it their rallying cry. I was still getting letters from mad Chicagoans years later."

The Sox clinched the division with more than two weeks left in the regular season.

"There was no excitement in Chicago sports until 1983," said Kittle, a Gary, Indiana, native. "The 1983 team was electrifying. The success, the exploding scoreboard, drawing 2 million fans. That was great for the city.

"I didn't mind talking to fans and having a great rapport with them."

The White Sox had plenty of time to set their rotation for the playoffs and succeeded in Game 1 of the AL Championship Series when Hoyt pitched a 2–1 complete-game victory at Baltimore.

Hoyt was one out away from a shutout when Dan Ford doubled and Cal Ripken Jr. hit an RBI single. But Eddie Murray, whose error in the sixth helped set up the White Sox's second run, grounded into a game-ending force play.

The White Sox still felt confident after losing Game 2 as off-speed maven Mike Boddicker beat them behind a 14-strikeout performance.

That changed, somewhat, after Murray hit a three-run home run in the first inning in a 11–1 Game 3 loss at Comiskey Park that got ugly. In his second at-bat, Ron Kittle was nailed in the right kneecap, and tensions mounted after Richard Dotson hit Cal Ripken Jr. and Eddie Murray took exception to an inside pitch.

Kittle was unavailable for Game 4 and for the remainder of the playoffs.

"I broke my kneecap," Kittle recalled. "I parked near the front of the park and not where the players park. I walk into the park on crutches, and Roland [Hemond] nearly fainted."

White Sox fans wanted to do the same after a series of mishaps prevented the team from playing a Game 5 with Hoyt on the mound.

The seventh inning of Game 4 was particularly agonizing, as the Sox has runners at first and second with no outs in a scoreless tie.

But Jerry Dybzinski, starting his first ALCS game in place of Scott Fletcher, bunted into a force play at third. Julio Cruz followed with a single, but Dybzinski kept rounding second and was too late to notice that third-base coach Jim Leyland held Vance Law at third.

Law was caught in a rundown. The runners moved up one base on a balk, but Rudy Law flied to left to end the inning.

Dybzinski started a two-out rally in the ninth with a single but was stranded at third when Rudy Law struck out.

Meanwhile, La Russa stuck with Britt Burns to start the tenth inning. Burns had given up just five hits but had hurled 142 pitches. With one out, Tito Landrum launched a homer to left that stunned the White Sox fans, and two more runs off Salome Barojas smashed any chance of fulfilling their World Series dream.

"Britt pitched so well with that [bad] hip," Walker said. "I don't know how many pitches he threw [150], but it was unbelievable. And he was limping every inning.

"We had the feeling if we win that game, we have LaMarr going in Game 5 and then Baltimore ended up winning the World Series fairly easily. It was almost as if we had won Game 4, we had a legitimate shot at winning the World Series."

KITTY KAT

As a northern Indiana native, Ron Kittle was more than the local kid who did well.

Kittle had a cult following for several reasons. He grew up in Gary and worked as an ironworker before becoming a full-time baseball player.

"The challenge kept me going," Kittle said. "I liked ironworking five times more than playing baseball."

That's not to say Kittle didn't like playing. He resumed his quest to reach the big leagues even after getting released by the Los Angeles Dodgers organization barely a year after signing a minor league contract.

"There was an old scout who told me I wouldn't play because I wore glasses," Kittle recalled. "I took the attitude early that baseball is a business and I was playing with it."

Kittle's determination was sculpted by his father, James, an ironworker whom his son described as "a man of few words. He had no compassion."

"Slim," as some people called Kittle's father, possessed huge hands and would use them to toss a telephone if someone called for one of Ron's sisters during dinner.

"I always said my dad invented the first mobile phone," Kittle chuckled.

But a local tryout in which he hit several tape-measure home runs at the old Comiskey Park easily convinced owner Bill Veeck to sign Kittle after he recovered from neck surgery that shortened his career with the Dodgers.

That was just the beginning of Kittle's comeback, as teammate and roommate Greg Walker recalled.

"It's funny, when I first met Kitty, I went back to A-Ball and was fairly disappointed about that," Walker recalled. "But he went to A-Ball as a third-string catcher when we started in Appleton, and he didn't play.

"Somebody got hurt and he started catching, and started hitting a little bit, and they started finding places for him to play. The thing about Kitty was that he ran pretty well for a big man."

At the same time, Walker, his wife, Carmen, and their infant daughter, Kaycee, lived in an apartment complex next to Kittle.

When Walker and Kittle weren't rooming on the road, Kittle would serve as a babysitter so the Walkers could have some private time. The families became close, and Walker and Kittle arrived in Chicago about the same time in 1982.

With different personalities.

While Walker is pleasantly reserved, Kittle's personality shifted gears and he maintained a strong bond with the fans.

"The thing about it is when we roomed together, he was very quiet in a room," Walker recalled. "But as soon as the door opened, here came Big Ron Kittle. How could the fans not like him?"

Ron Kittle slugged 35 home runs in 1983 and took home the AL Rookie of the Year Award.

The hype was well deserved, since Kittle hit 50 home runs in 1982 with Triple-A Edmonton. Kittle didn't disappoint once he reached the majors, earning 1983 American League Rookie of the Year honors by slugging 35 home runs and driving in 100.

Although injuries and strikeouts limited his development, fans still greet Kittle warmly during his visits to U.S. Cellular Field.

"It was a great story, and he's an outgoing guy with a big personality and they loved him," Walker said. "He got off to a great start as Rookie of the Year and made the All-Star team, we got in the playoffs...how could he not be popular?"

GREG WALKER

Jerry Krause was as much of a salesman as he was a superscout. As late as 1984, a year before joining the Bulls, Krause could scout a junior-college game in San Mateo, California, then make the 15-minute drive to Stanford to watch a game between the Cardinal and UCLA featuring first-round pick Shane Mack.

Krause knew where to look for potential surpluses in other organizations. In the fall of 1979, Krause took a deep look at Philadelphia's farm system in the Instructional League. This was the Dallas Green era during which the Phillies later lost the likes of George Bell to Toronto through the Rule V Draft.

"I was sitting in Roland's office when we got that stuff," said Krause, referring to the organizational rosters of every major league team. "I told Roland the Phillies left a prospect on a Double-A roster."

Hemond asked about the player and was told about a left-handed-hitting first baseman with power who was only 21. Acquiring this player would cost the White Sox $12,000.

"Roland says, 'Okay, genius. How are we going to get $12,000?' They weren't giving us anything to spend," Krause recalled.

After thinking about his options, Krause suggested he and Hemond scamper to the Bard's Room to see owner Bill Veeck, who was sitting with Rudie Schaffer, an innovative team executive.

Krause concocted a wild story that stretched the imagination of the executives.

"We just saved you $38,000," Krause declared to Veeck and Schaffer.

"I told him, 'I just came back from Arizona State,'" Krause recalled. "'I just got back from Stanford. Then I saw a left-handed-hitting first baseman. The son of a bitch can hit. He's 21 years old. He wants $50,000. We're going to need $50,000 to sign this sucker. Bill, can you give it to me?"

Veeck tells Krause that the club doesn't have $50,000, so Krause asks for $12,000 and tells his boss about a savings of $38,000.

A stunned Veeck asks how can Krause sign a guy and save money.

"He's on a Double-A roster. Bill, we're going to draft him for $12,000," Krause told Veeck.

Krause got his man—Greg Walker.

THE BLACK SOX SCANDAL

Enter any major league clubhouse, and you'll be greeted by a sign that warns players and other team employees about the dangers of being caught breaking the law.

Those violations include use of performance-enhancing drugs, illegal drugs—and gambling.

Major League Baseball, with cooperation from the Major League Baseball Players Association and pressure from government officials, has instituted strict drug-testing laws since reaching an agreement that avoided a players' strike in September 2002.

Baseball also moved forward after a drug scandal in the mid-1980s.

And, with the exception of banning all-time hit leader Pete Rose, MLB has survived gambling problems.

But it came at a cost—the 1919 Black Sox Scandal.

Nearly five decades before Ken "Hawk" Harrelson had his feuds with Kansas City Athletics owner Charles O. Finley and more than half a century before Finley unsuccessfully tried to sell the likes of Vida Blue and Joe Rudi for millions of dollars to pennant contenders, higher stakes were percolating on the South Side.

The scandal that scarred the White Sox for decades still generates plenty of interest, as evidenced by the fact that the legal documents from the 1919 team were auctioned off to the Chicago

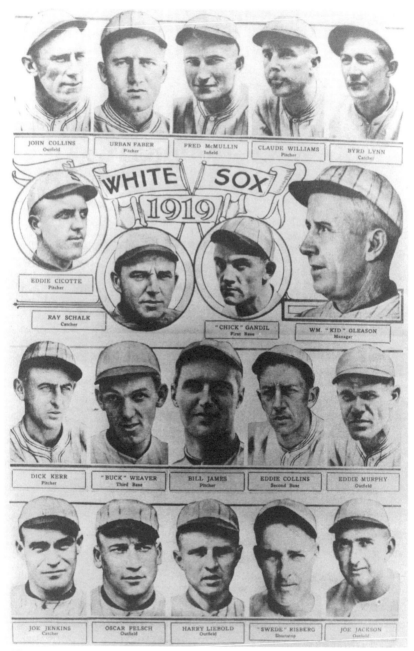

The 1919 White Sox, the most infamous team in baseball history.

History Museum for $100,000, topping 35 other offers nearly 90 years after the debacle.

Peter Alter, a curator at the Chicago History Museum, told the *Chicago Tribune* that it's quite unusual to have a large collection of documents on such a historical and scandalous topic.

The papers outline how the seeds for fixing the 1919 World Series were allegedly planted by gamblers from Boston, New York, and St. Louis.

According to several baseball historians, White Sox owner Charles A. Comiskey didn't share the same generosity to his players that he did to influential professionals, politicians, reporters, and other well-heeled people.

A plan to throw the World Series already was in the works before the White Sox won the American League title by 3.5 games. Those players who were allegedly involved or knew of the plot included Edward Cicotte, Claude "Lefty" Williams, Arnold "Chick" Gandil, Charles "Swede" Risberg, Fred McMullin, George "Buck" Weaver, Oscar "Happy" Felsch, and "Shoeless" Joe Jackson

While it is extremely difficult to imagine such a ploy being attempted in today's game—especially with rookies making a minimum $400,000 salary for playing a full year in the majors—times were extremely different in the Black Sox era.

It wasn't uncommon for players to work in the off-season—in fact, Jackson took a job in the Delaware Naval Yards during the war-shortened 1918 season, bypassing a chance to serve his country in France. And winning a World Series wasn't going to make the players financially comfortable, unlike today's champions that seem very liberal about sharing the pool from gate receipts: for example, several Arizona Diamondbacks clubhouse attendants were able to put down payments on houses after gracious players voted them full shares after their 2001 World Series victory.

But in this case, the players were allegedly fed up with not being compensated fairly for their achievements.

Game 1 starter Eddie Cicotte, who won 29 games during the regular season while posting a 1.82 ERA, suffered a 9–1 series-opening loss at Cincinnati in which the Reds scored five runs in the fourth. Cicotte allegedly received $10,000 from the gamblers before the game and hid the money in the lining of his sports coat.

The biggest tipoff allegedly occurred when Cicotte hit the first batter of the game.

Williams, a 23-game winner known for his control, walked three in the fourth inning that led to three runs and a 4–2 loss in Game 2. Williams had walked only 58 in 297 innings during the regular season.

The Sox eventually fell behind 4–1 in the Series before winning Games 6 and 7, and then were eliminated after a 10–5 home loss in Game 8 that looked only somewhat close because of a four-run eighth.

The scandal became public toward the end of the 1920 season that saw the White Sox finish two games out of first.

Although the eight players were acquitted in a 1921 Cook County Circuit Court criminal trial, federal judge Kenesaw Mountain Landis permanently banned the players. This case had long-term ramifications for the shape of what is now known as the Commissioner's Office. Decades before the office took a hard stand on Pete Rose, Landis made his mark as baseball's first commissioner.

"This was a seminal moment in history to look for leaders," said Jeff Idelson, president of the National Baseball Hall of Fame and Museum. "Their golden rule is, thou shall not gamble. This all afforded the Commissioner's Office to run a clean sport and have faith in the sport."

The Black Sox Scandal isn't ignored in baseball's cathedral of fame and history in Cooperstown.

"As a serious United States museum, we have a responsibility to the sport and to represent the game, for better or for worse," Idelson said.

Nor does the Hall ignore other historical black eyes. Idelson said there are many artifacts donated by Pete Rose, who is currently banished from baseball. Rose, the all-time hit leader, was found to be gambling on baseball during his time as manager of the Cincinnati Reds in the 1980s.

But before his stint as Reds manager, Rose developed his legacy as baseball's career hit leader. And before the Black Sox

Scandal, the White Sox won a 1917 World Series title over the New York Giants with the same nucleus that played in the World Series two years later—Jackson, Cicotte, Risberg, Gandil, Williams, and Weaver.

"Our timeline shows that it was a great team in 1917, a poor team in 1918 [finishing sixth and 17 games out of first place], and was a great team in 1919," Idelson said.

There are six artifacts from the Black Sox Scandal on display, including the jersey and glove used by Jackson. Also included is a letter from manager Kid Gleason to Landis, explaining why he shouldn't be penalized.

Jackson's shoes are part of a traveling exhibit. His alleged involvement tarnished one of the most impressive six-year stints by a White Sox player. Jackson batted .375 during the 1919 World Series but was alleged to have accepted $5,000 before Cincinnati's 5–0 victory in Game 5.

Jackson batted .356 for his career and .340 during his six seasons with the White Sox after being sold by Cleveland during the 1915 season. Jackson batted .382 with 121 RBIs in his final season in 1920 at the age of 31.

"The Black Sox Scandal evokes emotions in visitors," Idelson said.

For the White Sox fans in those days, there was a lot of permanent damage that needed to be healed and trust that needed reinforcement.

The Sox didn't return to the World Series until 1959, and they didn't win a World Series until 2005.

BILL VEECK

It's hard to believe that Bill Veeck actually worked for the Cubs at one time, but the ivy covering the outfield walls is an ever-lasting reminder of the influence he had on the cosmetics of baseball well before taking over control of the White Sox in 1959 and again in 1976.

His grassroots upbringing in baseball helped make him a favorite among the common fan. But by the time Veeck purchased controlling interest in the Sox from Dorothy Comiskey Rigney, he already had made a name in baseball promotions throughout his various stops.

In Milwaukee, he claimed to have moved the right-field fence depending on the power of the opponents' left-handed hitters. He also introduced Max Patkin as the Clown Prince of Baseball. In Philadelphia, he wanted to purchase the team and stock it with the best players from the Negro Leagues.

He finally owned his first team in Cleveland and became a civil rights pioneer in 1947 by making Larry Doby the first African American player to play in the American League, and later signed Satchel Paige to a contract that made Paige the oldest rookie in major league history at 42 years old.

Veeck won his only World Series with the Indians in 1948, but was forced to sell the team the following year to settle his divorce.

Two years later, Veeck bought the St. Louis Browns and messed with the deep-pocket St. Louis Cardinals by using little person Eddie Gaedel as a pinch-hitter and employing former Cardinals greats Rogers Hornsby, Marty Marion, and Dizzy Dean in highly visible positions.

Veeck had to sell the Browns after the 1953 season, following the purchase of the Cardinals by Anheuser-Busch.

By the time Veeck took over the White Sox, he had plenty of experience to keep the White Sox interesting in a two-team market.

It also helped that the White Sox were on their way to their first World Series appearance in 40 years, and that the excitement of the Go-Go Sox and Veeck's creative thinking dazzled the audience.

"Nine times out of 10, you could ask Bill, 'How are you doing?'" said David Schaffer, the director of operations. "And he'd say, 'Surviving.' That was his answer."

Schaffer's father, Rudie, was Veeck's longtime business partner and friend who introduced Bat Day, the first exploding scoreboard, and a picnic area at the old Comiskey Park.

Initially, however, Veeck had more trouble adjusting to the Sox's style of play on the field than relating to the fans who wanted a pleasant and safe experience at an out-of-date stadium.

Specifically, Veeck wanted more power despite manager Al Lopez's assurances that the White Sox had enough talent to overtake the powerhouse New York Yankees, whom Veeck enjoyed tweaking.

Veeck eventually obtained Ted Kluszewski from Pittsburgh in a waiver deal, but he didn't make a significant impact until the White Sox reached the World Series.

In the meantime, Veeck poured resources in making every White Sox home game a fan-friendly experience. He hired law-enforcement officials that helped reduce violence by 50 percent, despite a large spike in attendance caused by the White Sox's drive to the 1959 American League title. Veeck also authorized painting the exterior of Comiskey Park white at the cost of $148,000, and even assisted a staff of 300 to wash the grime off the seats that had built up over the years.

That was just a sampling. Responding to complaints from female fans, Veeck added more women's restrooms. The Sox also

Legendary owner Bill Veeck was always looking for innovative ways to improve the White Sox, a trait that made him one of the most influential owners in baseball history.

instituted Little League Days, and the exploding scoreboard and fireworks became staples.

Even a cow-milking contest became part of the promotions package.

"I have to say the thing that has disappointed me the most is the fact that normally now, it's cookie-cutter promotions," said Schaffer, who has an enlarged *Sports Illustrated* magazine cover of Veeck framed in his office at U.S. Cellular Field. "Whereas back then, we always thrived on the fact we created things, that we were original. Between my dad and Bill, you look back at all the things they did, and they were milestones. So it really makes you understand even how remarkable it was back then to continually come up with pretty interesting things that people truly did enjoy and that truly did work.

"There are a lot of promotions that don't draw flies. Back then, we'd double our attendance and more on some of those days, which was imperative to our survival. But in the same breath, it was very rewarding as well. It would give you the impetus to try even harder to create the next one. You saw the effects of it."

Unfortunately for Veeck, serious health issues caused him to sell the team. Veeck was thought to have suffered from lung cancer that spread to the brain, but Mayo Clinic doctors finally diagnosed that Veeck had suffered from a chronic concussion in which the blood vessels had stretched and put pressure on his brain when he coughed.

White Sox fans, along with Veeck himself, were rejuvenated when the former owner took over again in 1976—barely. Veeck needed to raise $1.2 million in five days for the American League owners to approve the sale from John Allyn.

Veeck took over shortly before pitcher Andy Messersmith won his lawsuit against Major League Baseball, a move that paved the way for free agency. But before Veeck was forced to sell because his limited resources prevented him from competing for free agents against corporate-owned and deeper-financed opponents, Veeck and his staff kept seeking ways to bring fans to the park.

Opening Day was particularly special for Veeck and Schaffer. In his first Opening Day after returning, Veeck, Schaffer, and manager Paul Richards re-created the Three Minutemen in the "Spirit of '76" by marching from second base to home plate—in full patriotic attire. Veeck represented the peg-legged fife player, Schaffer played the role of a drummer, and Richards held the Revolutionary flag.

In 1977, the White Sox celebrated Opening Day by issuing Wiffle balls and letting the fans throw the ceremonial first pitch.

"Opening Day used to be very significant for them," the younger Schaffer said. "They always wanted to do something that would grab everyone's attention and get the ball rolling for the season. They always tried to do something more remarkable on that particular day to set the stage for the year and get people's interest in the team."

One of those promotions was Urban Cowboy Night in 1980.

"The move was very popular and *the* thing at the time," Schaffer said.

Schaffer said they even had Minnie Minoso on a mechanical bull.

"It was fun to watch that night," he continued. "A lot of people came in with Western wear, and country-and-western bands and all that good stuff. It was a good night. Back then, as you could appreciate, we had to do things because the team was so pathetic that we had to do things that would entice people to come out. Otherwise, there was going to be another vacant night at the ballpark."

The witty ideas came from a small staff that sometimes involved the most unlikely people.

"Back then, there were 23 of us in the organization and that included [manager] Tony La Russa," Schaffer said. "It was one of those deals where after work, we'd all go in, sit down, have a beer together, and just be talking and say, 'What could we do this year to make it all exciting?' We'd start throwing ideas around, and that's how the idea of throwing the first pitch came up."

Pitching zany ideas was a way of life during the Veeck era, particularly during his second stint because of the lack of financial resources.

"The interesting thing was that we had no money," Schaffer said. "Our marketing budget, as I recall in 1976, was $10,000. So I think you'll appreciate where that stands compared to what's being spent on a daily or yearly basis [today].

"So the only stress was, 'How in the world are we going to pay for it?' But we always had such a good time that it was just fun for us to put something together."

Creativity also became essential because Veeck and company were coping with one of the oldest parks in the majors.

"I remember once we had a structural situation which was very serious and we had no money, and Bill finally said we have to sell one of our minor league players in order to pay for it, and that's what happened," Schaffer recalled. "You don't hear anything like that nowadays. But that's the way it was. It was so close to the vest we had to do extreme things at times to make ends meet."

Schaffer currently works as the White Sox's senior director of park operations at U.S. Cellular Field and couldn't single out one promotion during the Veeck era that brought him the most satisfaction.

"Just the fact that it succeeded, it truly drew people, was the satisfaction that I got from it," Schaffer said after a long pause. "Everybody contributed to the idea. I think we all worked together and if somebody screwed something up, nobody cared. Everyone would help them unscrew it, which was remarkable in itself for a lot of organizations.

"So it was just bringing that thing from a couple beers to fruition and looking at that and saying, 'Wow, we just brought in an extra 10,000–15,000 people because of what we created last week.'

"The remarkable thing is that I truly don't recall ever having one [promotion] that didn't draw. That's a wonderful thing, too. Nothing in particular, just the satisfaction and seeing the organization work together and bringing something to fruition that made people happy and made people come out, and you always heard from people how much they enjoyed it—which is all you can ask for."

LEAVING NO STONE UNTURNED

Of all the players who have played for the White Sox and crosstown rival Cubs, no journey may be as eventful or rockier than that of Steve Stone, who also has the distinction of serving as a broadcaster for both teams.

Stone was one of four players (including Steve Swisher, father of former Sox infielder/outfielder Nick Swisher) sent to the Cubs after the 1973 season in exchange for heel-clicking third baseman Ron Santo. Stone says he became the Cubs' first free agent three years later.

"In 1974, I was 8–6," Stone recalled. "I went to see [Cubs owner] Mr. Wrigley. I believed all that stuff about how Mr. Wrigley wanted to see all of his players. [General manager] John Holland wasn't giving me a particularly good contract, so I went to see Mr. Wrigley about it.

"He told me about his gum in 174 different countries. At the end of the conversation—about 15 minutes, which was nice of him to give me—I said, 'You know, I really came here to talk about the inability to get a contract that I think is reasonable.' He said, 'Go back and see John. I think you'll find him to be a little more accommodating.' So I got an $11,000 raise off an 8–6 year."

The following season, Stone posted a 12–8 record while hurling 214⅓ innings for a fifth-place team that lost 87 games.

"And they sent me a $2,500 [contract] cut in the mail in 1976," said Stone, adding this was Salty Saltwell's only year as the Cubs' GM. "I couldn't very well sign the deal after an $11,000 raise. So I'm the Cubs' first player to go without a contract."

Stone went more than two months without pitching.

"They wouldn't let me warm up on the mound before games because they said they were going to use me during the game, and they wouldn't let me throw off the mound after games because they said, 'We might need you tomorrow,'" Stone recalled.

"Finally, the second week of September, [hitting coach] Lew Fonseca went to John Holland and said, 'Why aren't you throwing this guy? What I saw today, he could shut out the Yankees,'" Stone said.

Stone pitched the second game of a September 21 double-header against Pittsburgh, allowing only one run on four hits in five innings.

Meanwhile, White Sox general manager Roland Hemond was in the Wrigley Field stands looking for ways to improve a team that was concluding a 97-loss season.

Hemond and owner Bill Veeck elected to bring Stone to spring training in 1977 and were besieged by questions about his health, based on rumors from the North Side about lingering shoulder problems.

"I told them my shoulder is fine and has been fine," Stone said.

Stone was offered a one-year guaranteed contract. But Stone was careful, because under the infant rules of free agency, players who declared themselves as free agents gave up their free-agent rights for five years. That was one of the reasons why the premier free agents, such as Reggie Jackson, Don Baylor, and Bobby Grich, received multiyear deals.

"Bill Veeck said, 'I'll make a deal with you,'" Stone recalled. "'I'll give you a guaranteed one-year contract. I'll also give you, written in this contract, the right to be a free agent at the end of this year. If you can pitch, someone has to pay you, whether it's me or someone else. If you can't pitch, I don't have [to pay you] for four or five years.' So I said, 'That's as fair as you can possibly be. I can pitch. Just pitch me.'"

Stone promptly won 15 games, made 31 starts, and threw 207⅓ innings for the South Side Hitmen. That made him one of the top free-agent pitchers, but Stone remembered how he was treated fairly by Veeck after questions arose about his health.

"I said, 'Bill, you gave me one year when no one else would. My father told me that in life, you always have to balance the scales. I've seen all your young pitchers, and they're not ready yet.

"'So I'll tell you what I'll do this year: I'll give you back one year. You give me my free agency at the end of this year—at the end of that second year—and you and I will be even. You will have given me one year when no one else would, and I've given you back one year.'"

Pitcher Steve Stone moved from the Cubs to the White Sox in 1977 and notched a 27–24 record in two seasons.

Veeck thought Stone's proposal was about as fair as a player can offer, so he met with the pitcher's agents. But instead of selling Veeck on Stone's 15 wins or other contributions, they asked Veeck to make an offer.

"Veeck said, 'I'll double his salary and give him $15,000 in incentive bonuses. You think he'd like that?'" Stone recalled.

Stone's agents agreed. Stone received a $135,000 salary, plus incentives at $5,000, $10,000, and $15,000 based on the number of starts.

"So I wound up making over double what I made the year before," said Stone, who was 12–12 with 30 starts and 207 innings in 1978.

In the midst of a fifth-place season that saw manager Bob Lemon fired and replaced by Larry Doby, Stone sensed that more changes were in store.

"I said, 'When you name Don Kessinger your next manager, I want you to name me your pitching coach,'" Stone recalled. "'Don is going to be a player-manager, and I'll be a player–pitching coach.' [Veeck] looked at me like I was crazy."

Veeck told Stone that he was going to interview Joe Sparks— now an advance scout for Oakland—and four other candidates. But Stone, who knew that Veeck would try to make a splash under the right financial circumstances, told him that only two candidates were capable of drawing fans to Comiskey.

One was Ernie Banks, but Stone said he told Veeck that Banks was more of a Cubs person. The second, Billy Martin, was already under contract to the New York Yankees.

"So you're going to come under the realization that you already have Don under contract next year," Stone told Veeck. "What makes more sense than to have a guy split a role, have a guy with a couple more bucks, and you don't have to pay a managerial salary?"

In the meantime, Stone said he was encouraged to test the free-agent market, but to come back to Veeck before agreeing to any deal.

The Baltimore Orioles, with an impressive blend of pitching, hitting, and leadership, came through with a lucrative four-year offer.

"I'll turn that down and stay with you," Stone said to Veeck. "You resurrected my career. You allowed me to win 27 games in two years. There are only 11 guys in all of baseball that have won more."

Stone said Veeck, however, steered him toward Baltimore because of their success under Hall of Fame manager Earl Weaver.

After falling one game short of winning the World Series, Stone gained tremendous personal success by winning 25 games and the American League Cy Young Award. He even started in the 1980 All-Star Game and pitched three scoreless innings (with current Sox broadcaster Ed Farmer representing the White Sox and pitching two-thirds of a scoreless inning).

"I saw Bill and Roland in the Biltmore Hotel [in Los Angeles]," Stone said. "Bill put his arm around me and said, 'I can't tell you how proud I am of you. How wonderful this was, the whole thing.'

"I said, 'It wouldn't have taken place without you. And I'll never forget that.'"

Well before Stone returned as a broadcaster in 2008, he remained grateful for the loyalty extended by the organization and the owner when he had trouble convincing teams he was healthy during the prime of his career.

"That's why the White Sox, specifically Bill Veeck, will always have a place in my heart," Stone said. "Because without Bill Veeck, I don't wind up in Baltimore, win the Cy Young Award. Without the Cy Young Award, I don't wind up on ABC-TV, which opened up my broadcast career.

"Without ABC, I don't wind up with the Cubs because I had no experience with the Cubs on television, I don't wind up as Harry Caray's partner for 15 years, and I'm still broadcasting because of the White Sox and because of Bill Veeck."

THE BIG HURT

O f the four first-round picks made by the White Sox during an incredible four-year span, Frank Thomas clearly stands out as the prime Hall of Fame inductee.

"I don't know how much more people can talk about him," pitcher Mark Buehrle said. "He'd probably have 40 more home runs [in his career if it wasn't for injuries]."

The blend of hitting proficiency and power made Thomas one of baseball's most special talents from the day he was promoted to the big leagues. After arriving from Double-A Birmingham on August 2, 1990, it took Thomas nearly four weeks to hit his first major league home run, but he was already holding his own with a .325 batting average.

Much of the groundwork was set in high school and at Auburn University—where he batted .403 with 19 home runs and 83 RBIs in his junior season—but Thomas admitted he continued to grow with added muscle and the supervision of hitting coach Walt Hriniak.

"All I had to do was work in the weight room and get stronger and bigger, and continue to work and be fundamentally sound with [Hriniak]," Thomas said. "And everything would take care of itself."

Had Thomas been promoted to the majors sooner, he might have won the 1990 American League Rookie of the Year Award. But general manager Larry Himes, who took great delight that Thomas was still available with the seventh overall pick in the 1989 draft, made sure not to rush Thomas before he was ready.

Thomas showed he was ready by batting .330 with seven home runs and 31 RBIs in 60 games. More impressive was the great patience he showed as a 22-year-old hitter, drawing 44 walks in his first two months.

The consistency of Thomas' offensive prowess with the White Sox was remarkable. From 1991 through 1998, Thomas was a run-producing machine, scoring at least 100 runs and driving in 100-plus each season.

In his third full season, Thomas set a single-season franchise record (later broken by Albert Belle) by hitting 41 home runs in 1993.

Virtually lost in the 1994 players' strike that cost the likes of Matt Williams and Jeff Bagwell a shot at breaking Roger Maris' single-season home-run record was Thomas' amazing season. Despite the strike that cost him the last six weeks of the season, Thomas amassed 38 home runs, 101 RBIs, 106 runs, and 109 walks while playing in all 113 games.

Those achievements helped Thomas win two consecutive American League MVP Awards.

Thomas was the major figure among a group of young stars that managed to re-create a winning tradition on the South Side during the 1990s.

"We had a special core that came in, all at one time," Thomas recalled. "Four straight years we didn't miss with great college players, and we set a

Frank Thomas won back-to-back AL MVP Awards in 1993 and 1994.

foundation and we had incredible young guys like Jack, Robin, me, Alex Fernandez, Wilson Alvarez, Roberto Hernandez, and Scott Radinsky. All of us came at the same time and set a core.

"It was a stroke of magic and luck for it to come all at the same time. We all got along well and played well together and started a winning tradition over there."

Thomas' popularity was so great that in 2005, rookie pitcher Brandon McCarthy bragged that he was a member of the Frank Thomas Pepsi Club as a kid who idolized the "Big Hurt."

"He hit from day one," Robin Ventura recalled. "Frank kept getting better and better. It was unfair at times. For such a big guy to be that powerful and that productive, he had to be the best hitter in the game for four to five years."

Despite Thomas' prolific hitting throughout the 1990s, the White Sox still couldn't regain the success they had in 1993. Advancing to the playoffs and even the World Series would have broadened the recognition of Thomas' achievements, and they eventually played second fiddle to those of Barry Bonds.

Thomas played in 346 consecutive games until suffering a stress fracture in his left foot midway through the 1996 season. He still managed to hit 40 home runs to go with a .349 batting average.

It also was the final year Thomas played first base on a full-time basis.

The move might have helped his longevity, as Thomas won his only AL batting title with a .347 batting average to go with 35 home runs and a league-leading .456 on-base percentage in 1997.

Thomas seemed isolated from a suddenly changing environment that saw third baseman Robin Ventura out for the entire first half because of a serious ankle injury suffered in spring training; the signing of fellow slugger Albert Belle to a long-term contract; and the infamous White Flag Trade that ended any chance of the White Sox catching Cleveland for the AL Central title.

Belle left in 1999, one year after Jerry Manuel's first year as White Sox manager. And it marked the start of Thomas' public feuds with management.

TURBULENT TIMES

Thomas stood as firm as a Redwood tree on a 1999 White Sox roster that lost veterans Robin Ventura and Albert Belle to free agency. But it also became a year of challenges for the White Sox slugger, who wanted to win while finding himself in the midst of a youth moment that included the addition of fellow slugger Paul Konerko, who finally found a home in Chicago after being a can't-miss prospect in the Los Angeles Dodgers system before getting traded in the middle of a 1998 game to Cincinnati.

Thomas was coming off a 1998 season in which his average dipped to .265 and his home-run total dropped to 29 in the same year Mark McGwire and Sammy Sosa seized the headlines with their historic home-run chase.

Injuries started to hinder Thomas' body as well. A bone spur on his right ankle and a corn on his right toe were the start of several ailments—as well as the first firecrackers sparked between Thomas and manager Jerry Manuel.

Thomas tried to play through the pain, but the results were too revealing to hide. On September 6, when the White Sox were closing out another second-place finish in Texas, Thomas didn't make himself available for Manuel's request to pinch-hit in the second game of a doubleheader.

Manuel didn't question that Thomas was hurt, but he was angry that Thomas didn't inform him of his unavailability.

If Thomas wasn't available, then Manuel figured there was no sense in having him with the team for the rest of the season. Thomas was sent home in the middle of a trip, and surgery performed a week later revealed that the spur had rubbed against the tendon.

In addition, a ligament in Thomas' little right toe had to be reconstructed as part of the process in removing the large corn.

The surgery revealed the pain that caused Thomas' ineffectiveness, but feuding with Manuel over his unavailability and being sent home didn't help his image.

Round 2 with Manuel started shortly after the beginning of spring training in 2000, with a prepared Thomas showing Manuel a doctor's note stating he wasn't medically cleared to perform the team's shuttle drill in which players run wind sprints set up at various distances to simulate running the bases.

Manuel ordered Thomas off the White Sox's practice fields at the Kino Sports Complex in Tucson, and then followed him to the clubhouse, where they began to hash out their differences in Manuel's office.

Despite Manuel's mild-mannered image and faith as a born-again Christian, he went after Thomas verbally behind closed doors with language that could be heard outside Manuel's office as the team was conducting drills.

While Manuel was angrily questioning Thomas' lack of leadership, the established slugger took exception to his manager—or anyone else—questioning his ailments.

After two hours, Thomas and Manuel made their peace after releasing the feelings that stemmed back to the incident in Texas.

The next morning, Thomas apologized to his teammates and stressed he wasn't quitting on them during a 1999 season in which they finished 21 games out of first place. Thomas emphasized he was "one of the guys" who could participate in good-natured ribbing in the clubhouse and was willing to jump in the foxhole with them.

This was the latest in a series of damage control statements made by Thomas, who got into an exchange with Ventura at Yankee Stadium during the Terry Bevington era in 1996 and needed to make a favorable impression on his newer and younger teammates.

Thomas' contributions, however, stood out most on the field as he led a potent White Sox offense to their first division title in seven years. Thomas ripped 43 home runs and drove in 143 while batting .328, and he also drew 112 walks to set up RBI opportunities for his teammates.

It was a season of redemption for Thomas, who was once again the driving force behind the White Sox's success. Thomas would have received more recognition had the BBWAA voters selected him over Oakland's Jason Giambi for the 2000 AL MVP Award. Thomas batted five points lower than Giambi but hit the same number of home runs and drove in six more runs.

That disappointment, however, paled in comparison to what Thomas endured at the start of the 2001 season.

On April 27, in a rare start at first base, Thomas injured his right triceps while diving for a ball. Thomas quickly left for Georgia to attend his father's funeral.

With Thomas gone, new teammate David Wells ripped the slugger for not playing hurt. The two sides hashed it out, but there was no way Thomas could prepare himself for the latest setback.

When Thomas returned, an MRI revealed that he suffered a season-ending tear in his arm, thus shortening his season to 20 games.

The injuries finally caught up to Thomas after the 2002 season when the White Sox invoked a rarely used "diminished skills" clause that threatened to severely affect his salary. That label became a constant source of embarrassment for the besieged slugger.

Thomas and the Sox finally agreed to a restructuring of his contract that included options for both sides during three years of his four-year deal. He also received a $1 million loan for agreeing to restructure his agreement, although Thomas' finances would be brought up later—by GM Kenny Williams.

PARTING SHOTS

Thomas rebounded nicely in 2003, although the Sox tumbled in the final six weeks despite Kenny Williams' attempts at fortifying the roster with veterans like Roberto Alomar, Bartolo Colon, and Carl Everett.

Thomas hit 42 home runs and drove in 105, but his most amazing statistic might have been the 153 games he played in.

Much of the anticipation before the 2004 season centered on how Thomas would get along with new manager and former teammate Ozzie Guillen, who wasn't afraid to call out anyone if he saw someone loafing or not playing the game the way he was taught.

Guillen, however, wasn't Thomas' problem as the two coexisted well. It was a left ankle injury that signaled the final stages of the Big Hurt's brilliant run with the White Sox.

Thomas already had hit 18 home runs well before the All-Star break, but the injury to his foot was so critical because his hitting style placed an emphasis on his front foot.

Thomas was lifted for pinch runner Juan Uribe in a 6–2 loss at Los Angeles on July 6 and was lost for the season. He also missed nearly the first two months of 2005.

The extended layoff was caused by an intensive surgery in which debris was removed from his ankle, a bone graft was performed, and two screws were inserted.

At the time of the injury, the White Sox were only 1½ games out of first place. But without Thomas, the White Sox were 41–42 the rest of the way and finished nine games out of first. Another disappointing season brought about radical changes in the White Sox's style of play.

The White Sox viewed any contribution by Thomas in 2005 as the equivalent of a midseason trade. The White Sox, already 33–17 without Thomas, regained the services of their slugger on May 30 and he went hitless in two at-bats before injuring his right hip flexor.

Thomas came back two days later, but his return was somewhat interrupted by six consecutive interleague games at National League parks that relegated him to one at-bat in a pinch-hitting role.

Thomas regained his power, as evidenced by his eight home runs in June, and he hit four more through the first two and a half weeks of July.

But inflammation in his surgically repaired foot eventually led to a fracture, and Thomas was lost for the year and wore a boot to avoid further damage.

"For a year and a half he was out," Buehrle said. "That's your career home-run leader for the franchise.... That can take the wind out of your sails."

Thomas' final at-bat as a White Sox player was a strikeout in an 8–6 loss to Detroit on July 20, but he continued to take his cuts

Injured slugger Frank Thomas threw out the first pitch before the 2005 ALDS against the Red Sox. Photo courtesy of AP Images.

well after throwing the ceremonial first pitch before Game 1 of the American League Division Series.

THE LAST LAUGH

As expected, the White Sox declined to pick up Thomas' option and gave him a $3.5 million buyout.

But they distanced themselves even further three weeks later when they acquired slugger Jim Thome from Philadelphia for outfielder and fan favorite Aaron Rowand and minor league pitchers Gio Gonzalez and Daniel Haigwood.

During the second day of the annual winter meetings at the Wyndham Anatole in Dallas, Thomas got off an elevator while in the midst of interviews with Minnesota and Oakland.

Wearing a jogging suit, he begrudgingly admitted it was time to move on.

"They did what they had to do," Thomas said. "I would have wanted my chapter to end a little bit differently.... I think I deserve that. I was forced to move on."

Thomas was more defiant at a news conference in Oakland to announce his signing.

"I'm shocked they brought in [Thome], who was more injured than I was last year, and they guaranteed him all that money," Thomas said at his news conference at the Coliseum. "I don't know where they went with that or what the logic was behind that. He had two major injuries last year.

"I love Jim. Jim's a good friend. But the bottom line is he's never done anything I haven't done on the field."

The White Sox acquired Thome despite lower back and elbow injuries that limited him to only 59 games with the Phillies in 2005.

"If I'm healthy, they'll be shaking their heads next year," Thomas said. "I felt I had been in the organization for so long, I'd get the benefit of the doubt instead of bringing in someone else.

"But [Thome] is a big left-handed presence and maybe what they wanted was a big left-handed hitter. It wasn't a better hitter, I'm going to tell you that right away."

Sadly, there's an old saying about people saying hello when they should be saying good-bye, and the White Sox and Thomas were never on the same page during the final years of his storied career.

Simply put, the White Sox needed Thome to balance a lineup that was dominated by right-handed hitters and believed Thomas' best days were behind him.

But Thomas never felt he was given the proper respect and targeted that slight toward general manager Kenny Williams, who actually gave Thomas the World Series trophy to hoist during the team parade.

"I think people, after a while, I did so much, start expecting more and expecting more and at some point what can you do?" asked Thomas, who batted .307 with 448 home runs and 1,465 RBIs in 16 seasons with the White Sox. "I really didn't know what more positive I could [have done]. If I didn't lead the league in something, it was like I had a bad year. It's good to go elsewhere and people can really respect what you do."

After agreeing to disagree with Williams in spring training, Thomas showed the White Sox and their fans that he had plenty of mileage left.

Before an appreciative sellout crowd of 39,354 at U.S. Cellular Field on May 22, 2006, Thomas got a measure of revenge by hitting a home run off Jon Garland in his first at-bat. Although the Sox went on to beat Oakland 5–4 in 10 innings, Thomas made his statement by hitting a second home run and a single off Garland.

That was a warm-up act for his mid-September coup de grâce that virtually knocked the White Sox out of postseason contention.

Trailing by three games in the AL Central, the White Sox needed an impressive showing in Oakland to gain some momentum heading into their final homestand.

Instead, Thomas hit a two-run home run off Javier Vazquez and drove in four runs to fuel a 7–4 comeback win on September 16. The next day, Thomas hit a three-run home run off Jose Contreras to highlight a 5–4 win. The Sox fell to five games out of first place and never got closer as they failed to defend their division, league, and World Series titles.

"I've seen it over the years," White Sox right fielder Jermaine Dye said. "When he's healthy, he's capable of putting up big numbers. He's healthy the whole year, and he's doing what they brought him over the do, and he's a big reason why their offense is rolling."

Thomas' 39 home runs and 114 RBIs raised his profile as an American League MVP candidate, an award that eventually went to Minnesota's Justin Morneau.

"Without a doubt, Frank Thomas should be in the MVP race," White Sox catcher A.J. Pierzynski said. "It comes down to big hits and when you get them, and he's got them at big times and he's got a lot of them."

The biggest compliment came the next day from, of all people, Kenny Williams.

"I let Ozzie and Coop deal with that," Williams said. "Suffice to say, I wasn't very happy with the plan we had against him. It certainly went against anything we—we above anybody should know how to pitch to him. But it's over and done with.

"You have to tip your hat to Frank for rising up to a big game for his team and the occasion. Hat's off to him in that respect. He's one of the greatest talents the game has seen. Aside from my personal feelings on the other end of things—everybody knows how I feel about that, but on this end of the things, on the baseball field, he's a special guy."

The 2006 season ended with Thomas batting .270 with 39 home runs and 114 RBIs and leading Oakland to the American League West title. Thome was just as productive for the Sox—42 home runs, 109 RBIs, and a .288 batting average—but the White Sox's pitching faltered in the second half and prevented them from at least repeating as division champs.

The following year, while Thomas was playing for Toronto, chairman Jerry Reinsdorf made a special visit to see him at U.S. Cellular Field.

"This is home," Thomas said during a return visit in 2008. "This is the place that made me who I am. There are still a lot of guys I know here, and they're family. That's just the way it is."

SPIRIT OF '59

Even after the White Sox snapped an 88-year drought with a 2005 World Series championship, the 1959 team that won the American League pennant is still revered by the Sox faithful.

"It was a great time for baseball in the 1950s," said left-hander Billy Pierce, who pitched that entire decade for the White Sox and lasted 13 years on the South Side. "Fans started to get into baseball and the White Sox, starting with the Go-Go White Sox in 1951, and they started going to the park and following the team. There was a lot of interest even before the 1959 season.

"When people remember 1959, they get very nostalgic. People remember it unbelievably clearly. I hear people say, 'I saw you pitch,' or 'Your team was my favorite.'"

White Sox fans had plenty of reason to revere the 1959 team. First, it was their first American League championship team since 1919, when the Black Sox Scandal left deep scars on one of baseball's oldest franchises.

The White Sox also dethroned the AL's perennial powerhouse, the New York Yankees, who won nine league titles and seven World Series in the 10 previous seasons. The White Sox had finished second or third in the seven previous seasons, including back-to-back second-place finishes in 1957 and 1958.

"It wasn't until the last third of the season when we knew the Yankees weren't going to be a factor," said Pierce, who won 20 games in 1957 when the White Sox lost a six-game lead in early June and ended up finishing eight games out of first place.

"The previous eight to nine years, we were always in contention throughout most of the season. We were always looking forward to the year it would finally happen," Pierce said.

The White Sox trailed by as many as 4½ games on May 8 before embarking on a season-high eight-game winning streak. They took the lead for good on July 28 when Pierce beat Ralph Terry and the Yankees 4–3.

With a team that relied heavily on pitching, speed, and defense, the White Sox were 35–15 in one-run games and were 12–3 in extra-inning contests.

Although there was little margin for error, nearly all the White Sox players felt strongly about their assets.

"We were a very good defensive team, but never scored a lot of runs," said Pierce, who works for the White Sox as a community relations representative and is heavily involved in Chicago Baseball Cancer Charities.

"But with the speed we had, the batter gets a better pitch to hit. Because of guys like Jim Landis, Luis [Aparicio], and Nellie [Fox], there was no question that speed helped us," he said.

Aparicio stole 56 bases and Landis added 20 when he wasn't robbing hitters of extra-base hits. Fox won the league's MVP Award with a .306 batting average, 84 runs, and 70 RBIs.

The biggest roadblock to the White Sox's berth in the

Pitcher Billy Pierce won 14 games for the Sox in 1959 en route to their first AL pennant since 1919.

World Series was the Cleveland Indians, directed by general manager "Trader" Frank Lane.

Lane, who was GM of the White Sox from 1948 to 1955, traded pitcher Early Wynn and outfielder Al Smith to Chicago before the 1958 season.

That deal paid off in 1959—for the White Sox—when Wynn won a team-high 22 games and Smith was the White Sox's starting left fielder.

The White Sox, as they did during their 2005 World Series title season, took care of the Indians in Cleveland. The 1959 team swept the Tribe in a four-game series in late August to expand their lead from 1½ games to 5½ games.

That sweep came shortly after the White Sox acquired first base slugger Ted Kluszewski from Pittsburgh.

New owner Bill Veeck wanted power-hitting outfielder Roy Sievers from Washington, but was talked out of it by manager Al Lopez. Kluszewski didn't possess the power he displayed in Cincinnati, but his presence made the rest of the lineup better.

"He didn't hit many home runs, but he helped us win some games in Cleveland," recalled Pierce. "In the final month, you could tell that he brought a left-handed presence to the lineup and made our hitters on both sides of the plate stronger."

Kluszewski went 3-for-8 in three games of the Cleveland series and batted a respectable .297 despite hitting only two home runs.

After the four-game sweep, the White Sox's lead never got smaller than 3½ games, and they clinched their first AL title in 40 years following a 4–2 victory at Cleveland that marked Wynn's 21st victory.

"We celebrated in the clubhouse, but we didn't get the full extent of what it meant to the White Sox fans and the South Side until we got home that night," Pierce recalled. "Coming home at the airport was fantastic."

Pierce and teammate Earl Torgeson took a cab ride from the airport to their Hyde Park homes. What they saw were people lighting flares on their lawns and fans staying up past 2:00 AM to celebrate a long-awaited title and the burying of 40 years of frustration and unfulfilled hopes.

"Everybody was outside or at a park," Pierce said. "You could see what the feelings were."

Since the White Sox had clinched in late September, Pierce already had sent his family back to their Detroit home so his children could start school. What they missed, however, was a scary moment for those who didn't follow the success of the White Sox.

City officials received permission to celebrate an anticipated championship with various noises, including sirens. That came as a shock to residents who weren't baseball fans and who thought the air-raid sirens represented an impending attack. There were several reports that residents scrambled to their bomb shelters and basements to prepare for an atomic bomb.

"I remember watching the game in my basement and recall Vic Power grounding into a double play to end the game," recalled Larry Karchmar, a Chicago attorney who was 11 years old at the time. "The air-raid sirens came on, and this was during the

The White Sox celebrate after clinching the 1959 American League pennant.

thick of the cold war. I was nervous. I looked out the window for airplanes and told my parents to go to the basement with me."

The celebration, however, helped Pierce realize what he and his teammates did for long-suffering White Sox fans.

"This team sparked a lot of fan interest," Pierce said. "We made a lot of people happy. You have to have a year like that where things go right. We played for one run all the time."

HEARTBREAK IN L.A.

The White Sox had the luxury of setting up their rotation for the World Series after clinching the American League title with three games left.

They also received an extended rest because the Los Angeles Dodgers needed to win three of their final four regular-season games—including a 7–1 victory at Wrigley Field in which Roger Craig hurled a 127-pitch complete game on the final day—to force a National League best-of-three playoff series with Milwaukee. In fact, the Dodgers were two games out of first place in the National League before embarking on an eight-game, three-city trip in nine days to end the season.

Los Angeles won the first game at Milwaukee 3–2, but trailed 5–2 going into the bottom of the ninth inning in the second game at the Los Angeles Coliseum.

The Dodgers rallied to tie the game in the ninth and won 6–5 in 12 innings. Had there been a third game, Craig would have pitched and would have had a chance to qualify for the National League ERA title because he needed only 1⅓ innings to qualify after spending part of the 1959 season at Triple-A Spokane.

Despite prevailing over Milwaukee, the Dodgers were overextended and couldn't start Don Drysdale or Johnny Podres against the White Sox in Game 1 of the 1959 World Series.

In addition, a hard-throwing 23-year-old left-hander who walked 92 in 153⅓ innings was employed only in relief until Game 5. His name was Sandy Koufax.

The White Sox respected the Dodgers, but Pierce felt his team deserved to be the favorites and the Sox played like it against

Craig, knocking him out during a seven-run third inning en route to an 11–0 victory. Kluszewski made his presence felt by smacking two home runs and driving in five.

Wynn capped the rally with an RBI double that helped him earn the victory with seven innings of six-hit ball.

"It was a relief to get on that bus, even after getting our butts kicked," Craig recalled. "I remember we got on the bus to go back to our hotel, and Don Zimmer yelled, 'Go-Go Sox, my ass.'

"They [the White Sox] were on a roll in that first game. It was mostly my fault. But it was no big deal because we knew we could come back. We already proved that just to get there and still had a lot of guys from that 1956 [World Series] team."

Indeed, the series turned in the Dodgers' favor in Game 2. The White Sox took a 2–0 lead off Podres, and they held the lead until the Dodgers scored three times off starter Bob Shaw in the eighth.

Charlie Neal's second home run off Shaw turned out to be the difference, although several fans remember a photograph of a fan accidentally spilling his beer on White Sox left fielder Al Smith, who looked up to watch the flight of Neal's first homer in the fifth inning.

But the White Sox's hitters struggled to generate offense after the first inning. They had a shot in the eighth, but Sherm Lollar was easily thrown out trying to score from first base on a double by Al Smith. Lollar had represented the tying run, but manager Al Lopez elected not to pinch-run for him.

"For some reason, our hitting stopped after the third or fourth inning of that second game," Pierce said. "We cooled off, and that play at the plate turned out to hurt us."

From the second inning of Game 2 to the sixth inning of Game 4, the White Sox managed just two runs in 23 innings. The lack of a clutch hit—despite 11 hits and four walks in seven innings against Drysdale—resulted in a 3–1 loss at the Los Angeles Coliseum with its radically asymmetrical dimensions.

The distance from home plate to the left-field foul pole was 251 feet, but it was 320 feet to left-center field. A 42-foot screen was placed to prevent any cheap home runs, but that still didn't dissuade hitters from trying to pull the ball. Craig recalled that

Left fielder Al Smith has a beer dumped on his head during Game 2 of the 1959 World Series.

Sherman Lollar was thrown out at home after trying to score from first base in Game 2 against the Dodgers—the Sox lost the Series 4–2.

switch-hitting infielder Jim Gilliam would occasionally bat right-handed against certain right-handed pitchers in certain situations to try to pull the ball.

To compound the White Sox's problems, Dodgers catcher John Roseboro shut down their running game by throwing out three base stealers.

"We didn't know much about them," Craig recalled. "But we did have advance scouts who followed them before the Series and knew they relied on pitching and defense and knew that Nellie Fox, Landis, Kluszewski, and Sherm Lollar were pretty good players."

Pierce pitched three shutout innings in relief of Wynn in Game 4 that helped the White Sox rally from a 4–0 deficit against Craig, who blanked them for six innings before fading in the seventh.

"Pitchers started pitching away from right-handed hitters to try to prevent them from pulling the ball," Craig said. "But I noticed that hitters were recognizing that and started to look for that outside pitch. So I would pitch inside and actually pitched better at the Coliseum than on the road."

Craig's ERA at the Coliseum in 1959 and 1960 (1.97) was remarkably better than on the road (3.22).

Despite solving Craig in the seventh, the White Sox's hopes faded when Gerry Staley allowed an eighth-inning homer to Gil Hodges over the monstrous left-field screen.

The White Sox, down to their final game, forced a Game 6 by beating Koufax 1–0 as Bob Shaw didn't allow a run despite allowing nine hits in 7⅓ innings.

That reprieve, however, was short-lived as the Dodgers returned to Chicago and scored six runs in the fourth inning of a World Series–clinching 9–3 win.

Despite three home runs and 10 RBIs from Kluszewski, the Dodgers were deeper and Chuck Essegian set a World Series record by hitting his second pinch-hit home run to cap the Game 6 victory.

"No one could say we backed in," Craig said. "We had to win on the road at San Francisco, St. Louis, Chicago, and Milwaukee.

You look at that White Sox staff and they had a Hall of Famer in Early Wynn, Bob Shaw, and Billy Pierce."

Pierce, who won 57 games over the three previous seasons, never got a chance to start a World Series game.

When asked whether he received an explanation from Lopez, Pierce replied, "No, not truthfully. I know Wynn had a great year, and Lopez wanted to pitch him as much as possible. It was just one of those things, but I did get to pitch in a World Series."

Pierce was selected to seven All-Star Games and pitched in four of them, but he didn't get a chance to start a World Series game until 1962—the first year he pitched for San Francisco. As a Giant, Pierce beat Koufax 8–0 in the first game of the NL best-of-three playoffs, and then in the World Series beat the New York Yankees and Whitey Ford 5–2 in a Game 6 that was played after a four-day break because of heavy rains in the Bay Area.

"Whitey and I warmed up under the [Candlestick Park] stands," Pierce said. "They brought in a helicopter to help dry the field. It was quite a thing."

Pierce pitched two more years before concluding a storied career that began with his hometown Detroit Tigers and ended with 211 wins, all but 25 of them with the White Sox.

"At that time in your career, [the 1959 season] stands out," Pierce said. "You don't forget it. Twenty-five guys bonded and played well together. You just don't forget those things."

Nor did his teammates forget his contributions, as Landis, Minnie Minoso, and Jim Rivera were among those who attended a 2007 ceremony that unveiled a bronze statue of Pierce in his signature delivery.

"They chased down all my mistakes," said Pierce, who was flanked by his wife, Gloria, their four children, and their five grandchildren on the U.S. Cellular Field concourse where Pierce's statue joined those of former Sox greats Nellie Fox, Luis Aparicio, team founder Charles Comiskey, Carlton Fisk, and Harold Baines.

RIDING THE COACHING CAROUSEL

TONY LA RUSSA

After joining the White Sox midway through the 1979 season at the age of 34, Tony La Russa has built a career destined to one day land him in the Hall of Fame.

La Russa is one of only two managers to win World Series with teams in both the American and National League (Sparky Anderson is the other). La Russa also is credited with popularizing the use of a closer in the ninth inning; moving his sluggers to the second spot in the order in an effort to get them more fastballs to hit; and placing a position player in the ninth spot to assure that formidable hitters like Cardinals star Albert Pujols would bat with runners on base.

Perhaps the biggest impact La Russa left on the White Sox, however, was the assembly of a coaching staff full of teachers that could help develop young players as well as aid veterans.

"That ended up as one of the greatest manager-coaching staffs put together," first baseman Greg Walker recalled.

Dave Duncan, a former catcher and teammate of La Russa in the Oakland organization, continues to serve as pitching coach under La Russa after starting in Chicago. Charlie Lau, who helped George Brett and others achieve their best years in Kansas City, served as the hitting coach. And La Russa was humble enough to hire Jim Leyland, whose teams battled La Russa's in the minor leagues while working in the Detroit organization, as third-base coach.

Tony La Russa was fired by the Sox in 1986, then went on to win World Series with both the A's and Cardinals.

Ed Brinkman, a sure-handed shortstop who won the 1972 Gold Glove Award with Detroit, served as an infield instructor. Davey Nelson was the White Sox's first-base coach and worked with the likes of Rudy Law to refine their base-stealing techniques. (Nelson also worked with Scott Podsednik in Milwaukee before Podsednik was dealt to the White Sox prior to their 2005 World Series title season.)

"I learned so much about how the game of baseball is to be played," Walker said. "Early in that season [1983] when I was scuffling, veterans gave me advice and that basically saved my career. After the rough start, I could have been sent down early and who knows what could have happened. But they took enough time to get me by and stay on the team and contribute."

One of La Russa's best traits, according to Walker, was keeping a tight bond between the veterans and younger players.

"We had team outings where if you didn't play golf, you had to attend anyway," Walker said. "It was a year in which Tony had it figured out, even at that point. I'm sure he's used a lot of things in his career that way, but he knew how to create a team atmosphere back then. It was a special year."

Ozzie Guillen appreciated the manner in which the staff taught the game and handled people.

"I grew up with Jim Leyland, Joe Nossek [in the 1990s], and Eddie Brinkman," Guillen said. "No one can be a better teacher of shortstops than Brinkman. And you can add Dave Duncan and Tony. Those guys were down to earth then, and Jim Leyland used to hit me ground balls, day in and day out, and it was fun being taught by them. And they taught the hard way. It's not like now, where the coaches say something to the players and all of a sudden, the players say, 'Ahhh.'

"You'd better listen to what they were saying. They say the wrong [stuff], and you say, 'Yes, sir.' That's the way I was. I was with a group of guys that wanted you to be great. They didn't want you to be just good. And they tried to take everything you had and squeeze you the right way to make you the best player you can be.

"You walk onto the field and Tony La Russa makes you feel as if you're the [greatest]. I was 21 and he made you believe like you can walk onto a field and you own the place. I was confident enough because the manager and coaching staff give me the confidence."

The White Sox held a reunion of the 1983 team in September 2003, and La Russa and Duncan had enough free time after a series against the Cubs to participate in a private gathering.

"I'm close to all those guys," Walker said. "It was a special feeling, especially to have Tony and Duncan stay after a Cubs series. There were a lot of special people in that clubhouse back then, and it was one of the big breaks in my career to be there and learn from them."

Unfortunately, renowned hitting coach Charlie Lau passed away before the 1984 season. Lau came to the White Sox in 1981 after helping groom the likes of George Brett and Hal McRae in Kansas City and later worked with Harold Baines. Walker said Lau's style was one reason he finally pursued a career in coaching.

"I had a great relationship with Charlie despite the little time I spent with him," Walker said. "That entire coaching staff was fantastic. But Charlie Lau was the main reason why I considered being a coach. I love hitting and love baseball, but I know what Lau did for me and other players. If I can be decent at it and affect people's lives, that would be a good profession."

WALT HRINIAK

There was a five-year gap between White Sox hitting coaches Charlie Lau and Walt Hriniak, but their teaching methods were incredibly similar. That's because Hriniak played for Lau in the minors in the late 1960s and adopted his philosophies.

Hriniak applied those once he became hitting coach in Boston and helped develop 1982 AL batting champion Carney Lansford (now a hitting coach with the San Francisco Giants). After 12 seasons, Hriniak joined the White Sox in 1989 and immediately made a believer out of Frank Thomas, the best hitter in franchise history. Hriniak was able to take a talented slugger like Thomas and make him even better without sacrificing any of Thomas' prolific power.

"When I got to the White Sox, Walt Hriniak just took me from day one and liked the way I was releasing [my top hand]," Thomas said. "He thought I was a two-hand guy when I got there, but I was already releasing. It was easier for me to adapt to his style. He just really got me focused on a lot of little things. He was the biggest influence.

"I saw so many guys he worked with. They were all high .300 hitters with power. So Walt was the only hitting coach I ever had who had answers for everything every day. And that's important. If you question why you're doing this, he's got answers. And if you're struggling, he's got answers. It was easy for me to be cloned by him because he had answers when things were going rough, and he'd have an answer when I'd go in the cage and work on something, and it seemed to always work.

"With Walt, you do the same thing every day and trust your ability and the numbers would be there. He was so right."

Hriniak left the White Sox after the 1995 season to go into private practice. But he often sneaks into the visitor's clubhouse at Fenway Park to see Ozzie Guillen and several of his former pupils, a gesture that Guillen treasures.

"Walter Hriniak was the glue of the bunch, and it was because of more than just hitting," Guillen said. "He had a lot of feelings for us. He knew us better than anybody, spent more time with us than anybody, and all my problems and players' problems went through Walter.

"Walter went through a lot of [stuff] in his career, and I remember a conversation with Walter that had nothing to do with baseball. There's no doubt Walter was the glue in that group. The good times and the bad times, and everybody trusted him.

"Maybe he wasn't the best for a lot of people, but it was the best for us because a lot of people trusted him, and he made a lot of people believe we were good."

FROM LA RUSSA TO FREGOSI

Tony La Russa was only 12 games over .500 from the time he took over for Don Kessinger midway through the 1979 season until Hawk Harrelson fired him midway through the 1986 season.

La Russa won only one division title with the White Sox, but would go on to have greater success in Oakland (four division titles, three league championships, and a World Series title) and St. Louis (six division titles, two league championships, and a 2006 World Series title).

Jim Fregosi, his replacement with the Sox, had won an American League West title with the California Angels in 1979. After three fifth-place finishes in Chicago,, he was fired by GM Larry Himes following the 1988 season. Fregosi went on to win a 1993 NL title in Philadelphia and broke the .500 mark in each of his two seasons as manager in Toronto (1999–2000).

"Jim Fregosi is a good baseball man and a friend of mine," Walker said. "But when you break in with a guy like Tony, and he treats you like a son.... Tony's career speaks for itself. He was young then, and had a huge desire to win. Losing a baseball game might hurt that man more than any person I've been around in the game. I've been around some great competitors in this game. But it actually hurts his gut to lose a spring-training game. That's how bad he wants to win. He'll be a Hall of Fame manager."

Walker enjoyed being around Fregosi as well.

Manager Jim Fregosi had a tough act to follow after Tony La Russa was fired in 1986.

"He didn't have a really good team to manage," Walker said. "We weren't that good, but Jim made us play hard. He was a fun guy to be around, and a good manager. His name still gets mentioned when a manager's opening comes up."

Ozzie Guillen loved Fregosi's "old school" style but said that style didn't translate well to players who weren't used to blunt assessments or were simply used to La Russa.

"Fregosi didn't put up with any [stuff], and maybe that cost him his job," Guillen said. "I never thought guys didn't like him that much, at least until five years ago when I talked to a couple friends."

The friendship and loyalty that chairman Jerry Reinsdorf has extended to his players also presents a delicate challenge, Guillen said.

"It's one thing that a manager has to be careful about, coming into this organization," Guillen said. "The players love the owner. Then the owners love the players. When you get between those two, it's not a good situation. You're managing Ozzie, Harold Baines, Greg Walker—good friends with Jerry.

"We didn't take advantage of Jerry. We didn't. But don't [mess] with the kids because they're his babies. It's not an easy situation."

UNFINISHED BUSINESS

Jeff Torborg was another White Sox manager caught between GMs. He saw a great future with the Sox, especially after his young team made a 25-win improvement in his first two seasons.

"Playing for Jeff was like playing for your dad because of the way he carried himself, the way he loved his family," Guillen said. "Jeff is Jeff, but in the meanwhile, he loved his players so much his players got away with a few things. He tried to avoid things. But I was lucky because I grew up with Jeff. I said if I got to manage, I'd be like Jeff Torborg at this particular time. But I will be Bobby Cox, just like that.

"I got my own stuff because I pick it up from them. You can be a manager and you see a problem, you have to wait before addressing it. Some managers jump, some don't say anything. Some see no evil, hear no evil, speak no evil. Sometimes you have to play games like that, but in the meanwhile, when it's over with, you see what happens."

Torborg was the latest in a list of managers who Guillen said helped him evolve into a leader and someone who would take responsibility for the team.

Jeff Torborg managed the Sox to two second-place finishes in his three seasons at the helm.

"Some managers, they kiss your ass and tell you they want you to be the leader," Guillen said. "All of a sudden you go out there and you say, 'I don't know what he's saying.' Then you're playing with different dominos."

Young players including Jack McDowell, Frank Thomas, Robin Ventura, and Alex Fernandez gave Torborg faith that the White Sox were going to be a force in the American League for several years.

Moving into new Comiskey Park and acquiring Tim Raines in 1991 were thought to have added energy to the franchise. Raines didn't disappoint, stealing 51 bases in his first season with the Sox.

But a disagreement over the use of Carlton Fisk—who hit 18 home runs and was named to the American League All-Star team, but also batted just .241 and grounded into 19 double plays in 134 games—was one of the reasons the White Sox didn't put a fortress around Torborg when the Mets asked for permission to talk to him about moving to New York.

According to one of Torborg's closest associates, the manager was told by a White Sox official that he'd be disappointed if Torborg didn't at least listen to the Mets' offer. The thought that Torborg would take the Mets' job to be closer to his New Jersey home made as much sense as batting Frank Thomas in the leadoff spot.

TOO EASY GENE?

Gene Lamont won an AL West title in his second year, and the White Sox were en route to their second division title—this time in the Central under the realigned three-division format—before the players' strike occurred.

This would have marked the White Sox's first consecutive first-place finishes since 1900–01, but that disappointment was only the first in a series of setbacks that concluded with Lamont's firing in early 1995—an eye-opening development considering what his teams achieved in a short span.

"The whole thing about this was that it was a totally different team after the strike," Robin Ventura recalled. "Gene took the blame, but the truth was we weren't as good [as in 1994]."

With a three-week spring training, the new players took too long to mesh to save Lamont's job. The White Sox lost their first four games, and a four-game sweep at Cleveland sank the White Sox to 11–20 and resulted in Lamont's firing after only 31 games.

At that point, McDowell had been lost to free agency, Fernandez was 2–4 with a 5.21 ERA, and hard-throwing Jason Bere was 1–4 with a 5.36 ERA. And in Lamont's final two games, the White Sox were beaten by 36-year-old Orel Hershiser and 37-year-old Bud Black.

"We never got it going," Ventura said. "Gene was a fine manager. He let us play."

OVERMATCHED

As a former manager, Terry Bevington was a pretty good third-base coach for the White Sox.

That's the highest praise Bevington could get, and it came from Ozzie Guillen, who had his share of run-ins with the overmatched manager.

To Bevington's credit, he had a winning record in two and a half seasons as White Sox manager (222–214). But his confrontations with his own players, an opposing manager (a spat involving Milwaukee manager Phil Garner that turned into a brawl and earned him a four-game suspension), and managerial mistakes hovered over him like a tropical depression that left a permanent stench.

"Besides Jim Leyland, [Bevington] was the best third-base coach I ever had," Guillen said. "But I think the [manager's] job was a little too big for him. He was insecure because he never played at the big-league level, and all of a sudden he tried to let guys know that 'I'm the man' instead of being backward and saying, 'I'm here, guys. Help me.' Then all of a sudden, things went south right away.

"When you try to be the man and you try to control everything, you're not going to have success. If you don't trust the people who work for you, you're done. And trust and discipline come together.

Terry Bevington had a tumultuous run as White Sox manager from 1995 to 1997.

"I think the Bevington era moved the White Sox back for several years. Not only on the field, but with the media and the fans—especially the media. The media has a lot to do with baseball. And I think the relationship between Bevington and the media was pretty ugly, and a lot of fans quit supporting this ballclub."

Even affable pitching coach Don Cooper, who filled in as pitching coach for two months in 1995, was no fan of Bevington during the Garner brawl.

"I remember being out there and looking to make sure everything was going right for our boys," Cooper said 13 years later. "I'm not a big Bevington fan. Looking back on it, I wish we would have at least let him get his [butt] kicked."

The lack of managerial control seemed to impact the chemistry in the clubhouse. In the midst of an 8–4 loss at Yankee Stadium on August 8, 1996, Robin Ventura charged Frank Thomas in the visitor's dugout shortly after Thomas struck out against Yankees reliever Jeff Nelson. Teammate Dave Martinez finally broke up the scuffle, and a teammate confirmed that Thomas declined to board the team plane to Chicago after the game.

It also wasn't uncommon for Bevington's players to be baffled by his moves. Bevington was known for calling relievers when there were no pitchers warming up in the bullpen. And early in the 1997 season, Bevington would employ a pinch-hitter for Harold Baines, who was coming off a .311 season and was showing no signs of slowing down.

That move didn't sit well with teammate Tony Phillips, who was heard sarcastically chirping from the back of the bus after one game while Bevington was sitting in the front.

"Tony was going to fly off the handle," recalled former coach Art Kusnyer. "I had to go to the back of the bus and tell him that was enough, that he got his point across."

Kusnyer, who had to step down after the 2007 season because of vision problems, insisted he got along with every one of the six White Sox managers he worked with, including Bevington.

"Everyone had their own style," Kusnyer said. "I got along with Terry. But I knew he had his problems with the press and didn't always see eye-to-eye with everyone. But I never told him or any of the managers I worked for how to manage."

UNSWEET SURRENDER

The White Flag Trade on July 31, 1997, symbolized the White Sox's frustrations during the 1990s. The Sox were only three games out of first place and had just regained the services of Robin Ventura, who had hurried back after suffering a season-threatening ankle injury in spring training.

The anticipation of a second-half run was detonated after a trade with San Francisco that sent pitchers Wilson Alvarez, Danny Darwin, and Roberto Hernandez to the pitching-thirsty Giants, who were trying to hold off rival Los Angeles in the National League West.

Despite the sight of valued scout Dave Yoakum at several Giants games, the White Sox settled for a wide range of prospects that included pitchers Keith Foulke, Bobby Howry, Ken Vining, and Lorenzo Barcelo, prized shortstop Mike Caruso (who would replace Ozzie Guillen), and outfielder Brian Manning.

"I was against it," Guillen said of the trade that virtually clinched his departure. "They [Alvarez, Hernandez, and Darwin] gave us our only chance to win. And we put all our emphasis and the hard work to win, and all of a sudden things were cut by a little bit.

"But now that I'm on the other side, I know they had a reason for it. But at the time, I don't think it was the right thing to do. They didn't let us finish up to compete."

Eleven years later, Ventura remains baffled.

"That was pretty low," Ventura said. "If I'd known that trade was going to happen, I probably would have had a different rehab schedule and slowed it down. But I don't make those [trade] decisions. I was bummed."

The stunning addition of slugger Albert Belle before the season and Ventura's comeback were offset by this trade, as well as by GM Ron Schueler's decision to sign free-agent pitcher Jaime Navarro instead of Roger Clemens.

It added up to another disappointing season and Bevington's dismissal.

NICE GUYS FINISH SECOND

Unlike Bevington, Jerry Manuel was hired from the outside, having served as coach under Jim Leyland in Florida and Felipe Alou in Montreal.

Profanity wasn't part of Manuel's vocabulary, although he didn't back off in occasional confrontations with Frank Thomas and umpires. Manuel's readings and recitations of Mohandas K. Ghandi and Rev. Martin Luther King Jr. symbolized his mild-mannered persona.

And although Ron Schueler, who hired him before the 1998 season, stepped down after Manuel steered the White Sox to a 2000 AL West title, successor Kenny Williams gave Manuel three seasons and plenty of resources to succeed.

Home-grown prospects such as Mark Buehrle and Joe Crede reached the majors, as did fan favorite Aaron Rowand.

Jerry Manuel led the Sox to one division title and four second-place finishes during his six years in Chicago. Photo courtesy of AP Images.

But surpassing the Minnesota Twins for the AL Central title in 2003 proved to be too difficult, no matter how many moves Williams made, including the acquisitions of Scott Schoeneweis, Carl Everett, and Roberto Alomar.

It's debatable among day-to-day White Sox observers as to whether Manuel would have saved his job with a division title. But that question was answered after the White Sox moved into first place on August 20 and held at least a share of it through September 14.

The Sox had a chance to expand their lead to three games, but lost their next two games against Minnesota to set up a first-place tie with 16 games remaining. Seven days later, Minnesota completed a three-game sweep of the White Sox at the Metrodome to take a 3½-game lead, secure the division, and seal Manuel's fate.

THAT '70s SHOW

According to Bill Melton, the seeds of the 1972 season were planted in 1968.

"It was all young guys," Melton recalled of the gradual infusion of young players, caused in part by trading away veteran players for financial reasons.

The young guys got a chance to play, but they took their lumps with nearly 300 losses in three seasons (1968–70).

The White Sox made a significant change by hiring Hemond and manager Chuck Tanner from Hawaii, California's Triple-A affiliate. Hemond was brought in late in the 1970 season to assemble the wreckage of a 106-loss season.

"It was a mess," Melton recalled. "Roland Hemond was selling players so they could pay the hotel bill. I remember Buddy Bradford getting traded. We were still staying in nice hotels, but most of us didn't know what was going on.

"I remember Roland came to watch us in Kansas City. He never heard of us, and we never heard of him."

That the White Sox were lacking in fundamentals made Tanner the right choice, especially with a coaching staff that included Al Monchak and Joe Lonnett.

"Monchak was a good teacher who made sure we did things right," Melton recalled. "You could tell right away they had a theory of teaching."

The instruction was especially important to Melton, who was attempting to make the conversion from the outfield to third base. Melton had a strong arm, but was flat-footed.

"Tanner remembered the same problem with Eddie Mathews," Melton said. "I was taught to move forward and that would give you better lateral movement."

Melton's work included fielding 1,000 grounders with this new technique. It enabled him to cover more ground, move more quickly, improved his foot work, and helped him to start more double plays. Melton would recall Monchak standing at second base to time Melton's ability to field and throw to second.

Tanner and Monchak were also trying to think outside the box: Melton recalls Tanner occasionally opting for a five-man infield in specific situations and setting up a rotation where each pitcher would throw three innings in a game.

In Tanner's first full season, the White Sox went a respectable 79–83. But Hemond sensed the need to take a big risk if the franchise was going to move into the upper echelon of the American League.

In a stunning move at the winter meetings, Hemond acquired controversial slugger Dick Allen from the Los Angeles Dodgers for left-hander Tommy John and infielder Steve Huntz.

The Sox would be Allen's fourth team in as many seasons, but Hemond believed Tanner would be a stabilizing influence. Allen grew up not far from Tanner's off-season home in New Castle, Pennsylvania. According to Melton, Tanner was familiar with the prejudice Allen endured in Florida while in spring training with Philadelphia.

"I never came across a guy like that," Melton said of Allen's talent. "It was all natural. He never came to spring training on time, but he was a great teammate. We could care less. We were all young."

Melton said that during the spring, Allen, unbeknownst to many, would work out at Sarasota High School at 6:00 AM with Joe Lonnett to stay sharp.

"He had a problem with the South, but he was like a brother to me," said Melton, a Southern California native. "He wouldn't go out. Joe Lonnett and Chuck Tanner would take food to him. He stayed at the Sheraton Sandcastle. We'd see [food] trays stacked outside his room."

Allen arrived at the White Sox's camp shortly before the end of spring training as the players were ready to embark on a strike that would wipe out the first two weeks of the season.

Art Kusnyer, who played for the White Sox in 1970, recalled the concern reporters had regarding whether Allen would be ready.

"I'll be ready as soon as the pitcher takes the mound," Kusnyer recalls Allen saying.

The acquisition of Allen became more critical when Melton, who would end the season leading the American League with 33 home runs, ruptured two disks in his back in a roofing accident at his home in late June.

"I was on deck in Texas on one knee and passed out," Melton recalled, adding that he underwent surgery in which no muscles were cut in hopes that he could return in late September.

"We were two or three games out in September and they thought I might give the team's morale a lift if I could play catch on the sidelines," Melton said. "I couldn't even move."

But Allen "changed it all," in the words of Melton.

Allen fortified an offense that had Pat Kelly, Carlos May, Mike Andrews, and Rick Reichardt. Although the White Sox hit only .238 as a team, Allen carried more than his share with a .308 batting average, a franchise-record 37 home runs (snapping Melton's franchise record), and driving in 113 runs (more than 19 percent of the runs scored by the White Sox that season).

Yet Allen preferred to stay in the background as much as possible.

"He wanted his teammates to get attention, like Carlos May," Melton said. "He would show up at 6:30 PM for a 7:00 PM game. He'd box around with Pat Kelly, and then start working.

"A few times he would take batting practice and hit the ball into the upper deck. He could run. Like [Willie] Mays, he could hit for power. He could steal bases like [Henry] Aaron, stealing them when the team needed it. He had great hands at first base. He was a fun guy, a team player who could take out opponents at second base."

Dick Allen was the AL MVP in 1972 and led the league in home runs, RBIs, walks, on-base percentage, and slugging percentage.

There were two staples to Allen's uniform attire. One was a helmet that he would wear on the field. The other was a long-sleeve wool shirt under his uniform.

"He told Goose Gossage not to be caught without long sleeves," Melton said. "That's why you always saw Goose with long sleeves.

"Dick Allen loved it in Chicago. He loved his teammates. We didn't bother him. He was the starter that no one bothered."

The White Sox, meanwhile, stalked defending American League West champion Oakland. After trailing by as many as 8½ games on July 18, the White Sox embarked on a 25–8 run to take a season-high 1½-game lead on August 26.

But the lack of offense finally caught up with the White Sox as they batted .225 in September and October and won only 16 of their final 33 games as Oakland pulled away.

That would be as good as it got for the White Sox for five years, as Allen's decline mirrored that of the club. Allen broke his leg in a collision with California's Mike Epstein while trying to catch a throw from Melton on June 28, 1973, and was lost for the season.

Tired of nagging injuries and increased debate about his preferential treatment from Tanner, Allen quit with two weeks left in the 1974 season.

If there was a consolation prize, it was the way that Tanner and Allen helped groom Gossage into a Hall of Fame closer. It was Tanner that convinced Gossage to accept a closer role that hadn't been in vogue in the 1970s.

"In hindsight, it was the best thing that happened to me," Gossage said. "At that time you didn't want to be in the bullpen. It was a junk pile where starters went when they couldn't start anymore. As a young man, you didn't want to be in that role. But Chuck, Johnny Sain, and Roland Hemond were ahead of the time in their thinking about relief pitching."

Allen, one of the most intimidating hitters of the early 1970s, encouraged Gossage to use his size and velocity to his advantage.

"He [Allen] hears me throwing, and he hears this pop of the glove, and I'm throwing aspirins that day," Gossage said. "Dick Allen stepped in. I go, 'God, there's Dick Allen standing up there.' He just wanted to look at some pitches.... He said, 'I haven't seen many arms like this,' and that's when he really took me under his wing. After that session of throwing, he goes, 'That's one of the greatest arms I've seen.'"

"We would talk for hours on end about pitching," Gossage said. "The value in that lesson...was how to make pitches and where to make pitches. I had great command of my fastball for a hard thrower. Even at a young age I could throw my fastball pretty much anywhere I wanted to. He would tell me, 'A right-handed hitter, that [front] elbow would be a target. You're going to throw the ball up and in, and as hitters this is something we really don't like.... The inner half of the plate, up and in. God can't get the barrel of the bat on a pitch if the ball is there.'

"My fear initially was if my body got in front a little bit and my arm was lagging, where does that ball end up? It ends up right here at their head.... Allen said, 'What's wrong with that? Every guy out there in that dugout is watching you, is watching what you're doing. They don't want any part of you, Goose.'"

VEECK'S LAST HURRAH

Shortly after Bill Veeck took over the White Sox again before the 1976 season, arbitrator Peter Seitz ruled that the reserve clause couldn't keep a player bound to one team forever, thus paving the way for free agency and escalating salaries.

The timing couldn't have been any worse for Veeck, who had to round up $1.2 million in one week just to purchase back the team he loved.

The White Sox lost 97 games in 1976, and all the promotional gimmicks made it seem worse. Veeck brought back Paul Richards as manager, but home attendance rose by less than 165,000. Minnie Minoso was activated at the age of 50, and Veeck's team

THE MILWAUKEE WHITE SOX?

Despite the White Sox's 17th consecutive winning season in 1967, home attendance at Comiskey Park dropped under 1 million for the second consecutive season.

With Milwaukee still stung by the departure of the Braves to Atlanta after the 1965 season, White Sox owner Arthur Allyn reached a deal to play nine games at County Stadium in 1968 and 11 games in 1969.

The nine games drew 264,297 fans, or nearly 33 percent of the team's home attendance that season. A May 15 game against the California Angels drew 23,510 fans—nearly three times as many fans as the Sox drew the previous night at Comiskey Park. A June 17 game against Cleveland in Milwaukee drew nearly 7,000 more fans than the White Sox attracted for a doubleheader against eventual American League champion Detroit the previous day. And the White Sox played a game against the New York Yankees (with Mickey Mantle at first base) that drew 40,575 fans at County Stadium on July 11.

Attendance at County Stadium wasn't as strong in 1969, and Allyn resisted inquires from car dealer Bud Selig to move the Sox to Milwaukee. Instead, Allyn sold his ownership to brother John and kept the White Sox in Chicago.

came out with shorts and collared jerseys that barely steered the attention away from the futility on the field.

Facing severe money issues, Veeck and general manager Roland Hemond got very creative. They dealt pitchers Goose Gossage and Terry Forster for slugger Richie Zisk.

"Unfortunately, Terry got hurt because Terry's stuff was actually better than Goose," said pitcher Steve Stone, who rejoined the organization as an announcer in 2008. "A lot of people don't realize that. Goose had a great career which culminated with his induction to the Hall of Fame. But had Forster stayed together, he probably would have been there right with him because they were the two best bookend relievers I have ever seen to this day brought to the major leagues, essentially at the same time. And in that pen, for the White Sox, to have both those guys there, wow. They were startlingly good.

"But when you're playing short on dollars, as Bill readily admitted, you can't do the things you'd like to do."

Finances also played a big role when Veeck dealt shortstop Bucky Dent to the Yankees in one of his best deals. The White Sox received slugger Oscar Gamble, pitcher LaMarr Hoyt, minor league pitching prospect Bob Polinsky, and $200,000.

Zisk, primed for a free-agent bonanza, hit 30 home runs and drove in 101 runs. Gamble led the Sox with 31 homers and hit .297. Chet Lemon had a breakout year with 19 homers and 67 RBIs. Lamar Johnson batted .302 with 18 home runs.

"I remember the pictures with guys around a Rolls Royce, wearing suits and gangster hats," Lemon recalled. "It was a fantastic season. The fans really rallied around us. It was a season I'll always remember. They were completely behind us. They let us know and they'd never let us settle down until we got a curtain call."

It also was the same year that organist Nancy Faust started a White Sox tradition by playing "Na Na Hey Hey" after an opposing pitcher was pulled in the middle of a game.

The White Sox moved into first place on July 1 and expanded their lead to as many as 5½ games on July 31 with a chance to take two from defending American League West champion Kansas City in a doubleheader and complete a four-game sweep.

NIGHT OF INFAMY

One promotion that was a little too "successful" has become one of the most well-known events in White Sox history.

And it had nothing to do with baseball.

In the late 1970s, disco music was at its apex to the dismay of many rock-n-rollers and others who didn't care for the dance music and the culture it had created.

At the same time, the White Sox hadn't capitalized on the success of the South Side Hitmen in 1977, as they went from 90 wins to 90 losses the following year, and the team was headed toward a steady tailspin in attendance.

Running on a skin-and-bones budget, the White Sox were known to combine a trendy theme with a baseball game to maximize their audience. As the Sox embarked on a 40–46 start, the anti-disco sentiment began to swell with the help of a young disc jockey named Steve Dahl. Recently hired by WLUP, Dahl was one of the leading crusaders to stomp out disco music. Much of his hatred was fueled by the fact that WDAI changed its format to disco music and made Dahl expendable.

One fan of both the White Sox and Dahl was a University of Missouri student named Paul Sullivan, who became very curious when the White Sox decided to stage a "Disco Demolition Night" where fans that brought disco records to be blown up between games of a doubleheader would be admitted for only 98¢.

"I liked listening to Dahl," said Sullivan, a Homewood-Flossmoor High graduate. "He was so huge, so different. He was ripping everyone, from WGN people to Mayor [Jane] Byrne.

"This was the time of concerts at Soldier Field with Pink Floyd and Emerson, Lake & Palmer. This was an extension of that. I was pretty comfortable walking around the park. It was such a terrible Sox team. I felt bad for Bill Veeck."

Admission to the game wasn't a problem for Sullivan because his father had season tickets on the first-base side. But the fact that Dahl was involved in the promotion made Sullivan even more interested in attending.

"I had just seen one of his 'disco sucks' concerts in Lynwood, and I was curious to see what was going to happen," said Sullivan, now a Cubs beat writer for the *Chicago Tribune*.

So after finishing his shift at an East Chicago, Indiana, iron factory, Sullivan and his friends drove to Comiskey Park and thought they'd have no problem with their commute or entering the park.

"We left early, but we didn't get into the ballpark until the bottom of the first inning," Sullivan said. "It was like a rock concert. We couldn't believe all the young kids that were there, and the place smelled like pot."

Even Sullivan was well oiled, courtesy of a pint of Jack Daniels he smuggled into the park that he mixed with a soft drink. His refreshments didn't alter his vision.

"People brought extra records so they could toss them at Detroit outfielders," Sullivan said. "I remember Ron LeFlore wearing a batting helmet."

Sullivan anticipated that the anti-disco event would attract up to 30,000 people, but the event was so popular that Sullivan recalls fans climbing the walls outside just to get in the park.

Finally the ceremonies began, and as records started to blow up, fans started to pour onto the field with little or no resistance.

"We jumped onto the top of the dugout and then onto the field," Sullivan said. "I saw them roll out the batting cage and light it on fire. Meanwhile, we passed around the Jack Daniels in the dugout. "

Detroit players like Mark "the Bird" Fidrych who took a break between games could only peek out of the tunnel to assess the damage. But Sullivan had an up-close discussion with a Tigers coach.

"Alex Grammas walked up to me and said, 'Son, give me that bottle,'" Sullivan recalled. "Then he said, "Son, get out of our dugout.'"

Sullivan chose to get out of the dugout—to go run the bases.

"I slid into home," Sullivan said. "One of my friends stole a sewer cap from the outfield, and he still has it. We were on the field for a long time.

"No team in the city had ever won anything in our lifetime. This was our only chance to run onto the field, and we were going to make the most of it."

That's as good as it got for a while.

According to Stone, one of the defining moments in the White Sox's 1977 season occurred in the second game, when manager Bob Lemon elected to rest three starters and fielded a lineup that included Jack Brohamer, Tim Nordbrook, and Brian Downing while resting a threesome that included third baseman Eric Soderholm.

To that point, the White Sox had tagged the Royals pitching staff for 22 runs in the first three games of the series, but they lost the finale 8–4.

"[A win] could have given us a 6½-game lead," Stone recalled. "Instead, they were able to make it a two-game swing by winning the second game of the doubleheader. Had we been able to beat them four straight, I think it would have made a bit of a difference. But hindsight is always 20/20.

"But I thought at that point of the year, our first team was better than their first team. Bob just thought it was time to give the bench players a chance. I know it's just common in second games of doubleheaders [to play backups], but my idea always has been when you have your foot on the throat of a team, and you get a chance, you best put them to rest."

That defeat started a four-game losing streak, and the White Sox went on to lose seven of eight, capped by a three-game sweep back in Kansas City that cut their lead to one-half game. The White Sox eventually fell out of first place for good on August 20 and ended up in third place despite collecting 90 wins.

"[Veeck] told me later on that if he had the money, he feels we would have been able to hold off Kansas City," Stone said.

Shortstop Alan Bannister hit .275, but he committed 40 errors, and backup help was an area Veeck couldn't afford to shore up.

Like the Yankees in the 1950s and early 1960s, Kansas City frequently spoiled the White Sox's hopes by winning four AL West titles in five seasons (1976–80).

"We couldn't quite get over the hump," Lemon said. "[The Royals] had George Brett, Amos Otis, Willie Wilson, Hal McRae, and John Mayberry. They had great players and were so used to winning."

A BOULEVARD
OF BROKEN DREAMS

There's a reason why so many tombstones had championship pennants planted next to them after the White Sox won the 2005 World Series.

That long-awaited championship ended an 88-year span of unfulfilled hopes for one of baseball's oldest franchises. Although many long-suffering fans weren't alive to witness the zenith of its modern history, their children and grandchildren honored their faith by decorating their final resting places.

But there was a legitimate reason for the release of frustration. The White Sox have never repeated as postseason entrants. They won a World Series in 1917 and returned two years later only to participate in the infamous Black Sox Scandal.

The most loyal fans waited another 40 years before watching their favorite team return to the World Series. But following that heartbreak, the team didn't return to the postseason until 1983, when they unleashed even more frustration after Tito Landrum's home run in Game 4 of the American League Championship Series.

"We were always competitive," said Bob Weisman, who, as an 11-year-old kid from Calumet City, thought the 1959 World Series was going to be the beginning of American League dominance for the White Sox. "Boston always seemed to have hitters in the top 10, like Ted Williams and Jackie Jensen. But it was the Yankees and

White Sox who were contending for many years because of their pitching."

But unlike the Yankees, the White Sox couldn't sustain that level of success for more than one year. In fact, after their second-place finish in 1920, they didn't finish as high as third again until 1937, when they placed 16 games out of first place.

There were signs of hope in the 1950s when the Sox finished third in five consecutive seasons (1952–56) and second in 1957–58 before breaking through in 1959.

But it was back to third place in 1960, fourth place in 1961, and fifth place in 1962. Even after Major League Baseball expanded to a two-division format in 1969, only once did the White Sox finish as high as second place (in 1972) before winning the American League West in 1983.

So what kept White Sox fans from jumping off the band-wagon?

"The Cubs were a complete embarrassment," said Weisman, now an attorney in downtown Chicago. "Until 1985, they would be lucky to draw more than 3,000 people. That College of Coaches [the Cubs' attempt to rotate the manager position among eight different coaches] was a joke, completely embarrassing. They were the equivalent of the Kansas City A's. How could you be a Cubs fan then?"

But watching the Cubs fall short provided only temporary relief from the Sox's continuous struggles.

"It's a thing you just grow up with," said Chicago attorney Larry Karchmar. "Growing up in the '50s and '60s, baseball was everything. I grew up on the West Side as a Sox fan. I'd take the 'L' to games and never give up on the team."

Karchmar once shared office space with Mark Lieberman, another frustrated White Sox fan.

"He became seriously ill and said, 'I just hope I live long enough to see a World Series,'" Karchmar recalled.

Lieberman passed away in 2004, one year before the White Sox won the World Series.

"But I told his widow that the White Sox won the 2005 World Series for him," Karchmar said.

SIXTIES SWOON

San Francisco general manager Brian Sabean, who finished first or second in each of his first eight seasons with the Giants, once said that the toughest thing in baseball is winning and developing young talent at the same time.

The White Sox were on the verge of doing that until shortly after the 1959 season. The 1959 American League championship was supposed to be a springboard for continued success at the expense of the Sox's longtime nemesis, the New York Yankees.

"From the players' viewpoint, we couldn't understand what happened after 1959," said pitcher Billy Pierce, who was dealt to San Francisco after the 1961 season and helped the Giants reach the World Series the following year.

The Sox's miscalculations started when they dealt first baseman "Stormin'" Norm Cash, catcher John Romano, and third baseman Bubba Phillips to Cleveland for 34-year-old Minnie Minoso, pitchers Jake Striker and Don Ferrarese, and catcher Dick Brown.

Cash, who was 25 at the time of the trade, was quickly dealt to Detroit and went on to win the 1961 AL batting title and hit 373 home runs in 15 seasons with the Tigers.

Romano was a two-time AL All-Star in five seasons with the Indians before returning to the White Sox in a trade, but by then his best days were behind him. Phillips gave the Indians three productive seasons before moving to Detroit to finish his career.

For the White Sox, Minoso batted .311 and .280 in his first two seasons but stole only 26 bases. Striker pitched in only two games and Ferrarese just five for the White Sox, and Brown played in 16 games and was sold to Milwaukee the following winter.

To replace Phillips at third, the White Sox acquired Gene Freese at the cost of outfield prospect Johnny Callison. Freese hit 17 home runs and drove in 79 runs, but was dealt the next season for pitchers Juan Pizarro and Cal McLish. Meanwhile, Callison emerged as one of the Phillies' best offensive players. In a four-year span (1962–65), Callison averaged 28 home runs and 92 RBIs. He remained productive through the 1970 season when he hit 19 home runs and drove in 68 runs—for the Cubs.

After pushing hard during the 1959 season to get Roy Sievers from Washington, owner Bill Veeck finally got his wish by landing Sievers for first baseman Don Mincher and catcher Earl Battey. Sievers hit 55 home runs and drove in 185 in his two seasons with the White Sox, but Battey promptly won the Gold Glove Award the next three seasons and earned four All-Star selections. He also finished in the top 10 in the AL MVP balloting three times. Mincher started a 13-year career in which he hit 22 home runs or more in five seasons.

The moves produced a third-place finish, 10 games behind the Yankees.

What was stunning to Pierce was that the White Sox elected to move Battey while 35-year-old Sherman Lollar was starting his 12th season as a full-time catcher.

"Sherm was a great catcher but getting older, and Battey was the No. 1 replacement," Pierce said. "We already had Earl Torgeson and Klu [Ted Kluszewski] as our first basemen, and they were both in their mid-thirties. And we went out and traded Cash and Mincher.

"All our replacements were gone. And age does catch up with you. I think he [owner Bill Veeck] figured a little extra power would do it [win the World Series]. He wanted power, and everyone has their own opinion."

THE CURSE OF APARICIO

Well before the San Francisco Giants traded Willie Mays to the New York Mets and before the Braves dealt Henry Aaron to Milwaukee, the White Sox coped with dealing their own homegrown hero.

Near the peak of his career, shortstop Luis Aparicio was traded to Baltimore in a six-player trade before the 1963 season.

"The Sox will need 40 years to win the pennant again," a bitter Aparicio declared.

It took longer, although the White Sox finally grasped the idea of acquiring young talent instead of dealing it away for a short-term fix.

In return for Aparicio, the White Sox received first baseman Pete Ward, who finished second to teammate Gary Peters in the American League Rookie of the Year balloting.

Although the White Sox finished 10½ games behind the Yankees, they built a foundation behind Peters and his 19 wins.

FROM WORLD SERIES TO SECOND PLACE

As a native Chicagoan who grew up on the Northwest side, was a multisport standout at Archbishop Weber High School, and appeared in eight World Series during his first 10 major league seasons, Bill "Moose" Skowron didn't have much left to accomplish.

But in the middle of the 1964 season, he got another challenge—he was traded to his hometown White Sox, who were in the midst of an AL pennant race against his former New York teammates.

"We lost the pennant by one game," Skowron recalled from a front-row seat at U.S. Cellular Field while watching batting practice. "We had beaten them four in a row [August 17–20]. That was when Yogi [Berra] was the manager of the Yankees, and Phil Linz was playing the harmonica on the bus. Yogi yelled at him to stick the harmonica.

Chicago native Bill "Moose" Skowron couldn't push the White Sox past the Yankees during the 1964 pennant race.

"And Linz said to Mickey Mantle, 'What did Yogi say?' Mickey and Whitey Ford said, 'Yogi said to play it louder.' And they got into a fight. That motivated the Yankees."

The Yankees, 4½ games out of first place at the time, won 11 straight in late September to overtake Baltimore and the White Sox, who won their final nine games but finished one game out of first place.

"That was the most disappointing year of my career, because we should have been in the World Series," Skowron said.

The Sox acquired Skowron from Washington in mid-July and he joined his new teammates in Boston. But Skowron, who had three hits in his second game with the White Sox at Fenway Park, disclosed later that he wasn't 100 percent healthy after leaving the Senators.

"I was in the dugout when Chuck Hinton hit a foul ball," Skowron recalled. "Eddie Brinkman, my roommate, was with the Washington Senators, and I put my hand in front of his face because the ball was coming and was going to hit him in the mouth. The ball hit me on the hand, and I wasn't the same.

"I don't know what the heck happened. I hit only 17 home runs that year, and I had 13 with the Senators before I got traded to the White Sox."

Gary Peters led a strong pitching staff with 20 victories, and no pitchers had more than nine losses. But the offense was challenged.

"That would have made my whole life," Skowron said of a 1964 World Series bid that fell short. "I grew up 30 minutes from Wrigley Field. I didn't go to [Comiskey Park] too much because we had no way to get there. I was always afraid. We'd catch a bus on Addison and go to Wrigley Field."

SLIPPING AWAY

Winning 95 games might not seem like the start of a downward spiral, but the White Sox finished seven games out of first place in 1965.

It was more maddening because the Minnesota Twins—not the perennial power New York Yankees—were the ones who had distanced themselves from the rest of the American League pack.

Pitcher Juan Pizarro's arm injury hurt the White Sox's pennant chances, and manager Al Lopez stepped down after the 1965 season.

Although Don Buford—a former two-sport star at the University of Southern California—and AL Rookie of the Year Tommie Agee combined to steal 95 bases, the White Sox slipped to fourth place in 1966.

And morale took a severe dip as well under volcanic manager Eddie Stanky.

"A few of my teammates—Eddie Fisher, Hoyt Wilhelm, Gary Peters, and Joel Horlen—said, 'Moose, we want you to play first base. Why don't you go to Eddie Stanky?'" Moose Skowron recalled of the dialogue early in the 1967 season.

Skowron pleaded his case to Stanky, stressing that he could still produce despite batting .249 with six home runs in 120 games the previous season.

"[Stanky] said, 'It's my prerogative,'" Skowron recalled. "I don't know what the word means. But I got traded the next day. Stanky said there are two teams that wanted me, the Cleveland Indians or the Los Angeles Angels. I said I'd go to California because Don Mincher was the first baseman, and I didn't mind being beat by him. And it turned out it was my last year.

"And Mr. Gene Autry [the Angels' owner] asked me to play another year. And I said, 'Mr. Autry, I don't want to play no more. I've had 17 years—14 in the majors and three in the minors. And I got to come home.'"

The Sox also were sent home despite being involved in one of the greatest pennant races in baseball history, as four teams finished within three games of each other. Being swept in a doubleheader by Kansas City was the start of the Sox's five-game losing streak to end the season.

That Skowron even wore a White Sox uniform was amazing despite his local upbringing.

"I think I'm the only guy who came out of Chicago who played at Soldier Field, Chicago Stadium, Wrigley Field, and [Comiskey Park]," Skowron said. "That's a nice record I have."

WHO'S TO BLAME?

Between 1984 and 2004, the White Sox produced several great hitters, Gold Glove–caliber defenders, dominating pitchers, and top-notch instructors, all under a stable and supportive ownership.

Yet that era produced only two division titles, turnover at the managerial and general managerial positions, and constant conflicts with players.

The underachieving started shortly after falling short of winning the 1983 American League title.

"If we would have won, more resources would have been there, and we followed it up with a dud in 1984 [88 losses and a fifth-place finish] and probably set our organization back," first baseman Greg Walker said. "But I was so young, I was just trying to survive.

"Missing that opportunity really hurt the organization for a few years."

Many players and followers felt the biggest loss was GM Roland Hemond trading Jerry Koosman to Philadelphia for reliever Ron Reed, a move made to shore up the bullpen after Dennis Lamp left for Toronto via free agency.

"I don't know if any of us realized how important Koosman was to the clubhouse," Walker said. "[Hemond] got a good pitcher in Ron Reed. That was a missing link to the bullpen. [But] we really missed Koosman's leadership."

With Philadelphia, Koosman pitched 54⅓ more innings than he did the previous season with the White Sox and he lowered his ERA by more than a run and a half.

"If Roland had to do it over again, he probably would have kept the Kooser," Walker said.

TOO ATHLETIC?

Some White Sox players believe no matter how successful they were in the early 1990s, they were no match for La Russa's Oakland teams that won four division titles (1988–90, 1992) and a league title in 1990, when the White Sox won 94 games but finished second in the AL West.

"Believe me, I don't think we knew what the [bleep] we were doing," Guillen said. "We just played. We didn't know if we were in the pennant race or not. If you compete against Oakland, holy [bleep].... The Oakland team had maybe four Hall of Famers. But we just go out and play the best we can."

The White Sox's signature moment that season came on June 24, 1990, during an eight-game winning streak. Jack McDowell engaged in some good-natured bench-jockeying that rattled the A's Dave Stewart, who came back to start the tenth inning but gave up a game-winning home run to Dan Pasqua to cap the Sox's three-game sweep.

"We're not afraid of anything," Guillen said. "No one tried to intimidate us. I think Jack was a bad mother[bleeper]. Jack, when he said something on the field, Jack was the first one to step it up and call bull[bleep]."

But the White Sox never took sole possession of first place and Oakland got on one of its patented runs to easily pull away.

"Oakland was in their heyday," Robin Ventura said. "It wasn't an easy division. Minnesota won the World Series the following year [1991]. And when they went to a three-division format, we had our battles with Cleveland."

Guillen believes the wild-card berth came about five years too late.

"I was talking in Oakland with a couple kids on the bench [in August 2008] and now when you're two games over .500, you're in the pennant race," Guillen said. "Back then, you play two games over .500, you're in last place."

Another theory was that the White Sox didn't add enough talent to overtake Oakland, which acquired second baseman Willie Randolph from the Los Angeles Dodgers in May 1990 and then added Harold Baines and Willie McGee in separate deals before the August 31 deadline.

"I look at this time now, I tell people that if Jerry [Reinsdorf] opened up that purse the way he did nowadays, we'd have four or five championships back then," Frank Thomas said. "But we didn't. He knew we had a strong young core of guys and could almost get to the next level. But we didn't get it done."

A SEASON TO FORGET

The White Sox's 2007 season-in-review guide featured closer Bobby Jenks hoisting his right arm after tying a major league record by retiring 41 consecutive batters, Mark Buehrle celebrating his no-hitter against Texas, and Jim Thome watching the flight of his 500th career home run.

That was the extent of the White Sox's highlights during a 72–90 season that placed them fourth in the American League Central, marking their lowest overall finish since placing seventh in 1989.

The Sox were in last place in the AL Central with 11 games left.

The offense finished last in the AL in batting average (.246), runs (693), and on-base percentage (.318).

In a season of many low points, one of them occurred on July 21 during the seventh inning of an 11–2 loss at Boston on national television. Three relievers combined to walk five consecutive batters during a seven-run inning.

"I can't even say it's disappointing anymore," manager Ozzie Guillen said. "I think it was funny. We are on national TV. I was making fun of Coop [pitching coach Don Cooper]. I said, 'When you go out there, make sure they know who the pitching coach of this ballclub is.'"

ACKNOWLEDGMENTS

This project wouldn't have been completed without the amazing cooperation of so many people.

First, a tip of the cap to my fellow *Chicago Tribune* coworkers, particularly Dan McGrath, Dave van Dyck, and Paul Sullivan, for their support and knowledge. Tom Bast and Adam Motin of Triumph Books displayed tremendous patience in getting this book started and completed.

The entire White Sox organization, from front-office staffers to uniform members to former players, were extremely cooperative. Ed Cassin, the director of travel, and Scott Reifert, Bob Beghtol, and Pat O'Connell were accommodating in fulfilling my requests.

My fellow competitors on the White Sox's beat provided depth to some incidents that occurred shortly before I arrived in Chicago in 2005. Scot Gregor of the *Daily Herald*, who has covered the White Sox since 1993, was a great resource. So were veteran radio personalities Chet Coppock and Bruce Levine, as well as Baseball America's Jim Callis.

Since I started in the newspaper business in September 1980, I quickly learned to appreciate the work and observations of hundreds of baseball scouts, especially those who travel great distances and evaluate talent in less-than-ideal conditions.

There are at least six amateur coaches who set a good example for their student-athletes and have been nice enough to share their knowledge with me over several years—Dave Currie of Wilcox High School in Santa Clara, California; Bill Hutton of Archbishop Mitty High in San Jose, California; Dave Lawn of Servite High in Anaheim, California; Sam Piraro of San Jose State University; Mark Marquess of Stanford; and Mike Gillespie of UC Irvine.

But the greatest support starts at home, and I'm lucky to have the greatest parents in the world, as well as two sisters and a brother who tolerated me during my mercurial youth. And what can be better than to have a wife like my Nanci who is married to me *and* raises me? I guess it helps to be married into a family whose allegiances to the White Sox and Cubs are split like the great city of Chicago.

SOURCES

Books

Chicago White Sox 2005 Media Guide.

Chicago White Sox 2006 Media Guide.

Chicago White Sox 2008 Media Guide.

Freedman, Lew, and Billy Pierce. *Then Harold Said to Ozzie....* Chicago: Triumph Books, 2007.

Lindberg, Richard C., and Mark Fletcher. *Total White Sox*. Chicago: Triumph Books, 2006.

Veeck, Bill, and Ed Linn. *Veeck As In Wreck*. Chicago: University of Chicago Press, 2001.

Piersall, Jimmy, and Richard Whittingham. *The Truth Hurts*. Chicago: Contemporary Books, 1984.

Periodicals

Arizona Daily Star

Chicago Sun-Times

Chicago Tribune

Daily Southtown

Dallas Morning News

Sports Illustrated

Websites

baseballamerica.com

baseballhalloffame.com

baseball-reference.com
mlb.com
retrosheet.org
thebaseballcube.com